Hell's Heaven

A Metamorphosis In Costa Rica

ANTHONY FLORENCE

BALBOA.PRESS
A DIVISION OF HAY HOUSE

Balboa Press books may be ordered through booksellers or by contacting:

Balboa Press
A Division of Hay House
1663 Liberty Drive
Bloomington, IN 47403
www.balboapress.com
844-682-1282

Print information available on the last page.

ISBN: 978-1-9822-7212-8 (sc)
ISBN: 978-1-9822-7214-2 (hc)
ISBN: 978-1-9822-7213-5 (e)

Library of Congress Control Number: 2021916040

Balboa Press rev. date: 08/25/2021

I wouldn't give my life back for the world.
I just don't ever want to do it again.

Contents

Prologue

I can't believe it! Is this really happening? This place is for my siblings, not me! I didn't have time to pinch myself before the officer asked me, *"¿Regala me tus zapatos o cordones?"* (Do you want to give me your shoes or shoestrings?)

I looked down at the coating of contaminated water puddles that dominated the cell floor and sarcastically answered, *"Mis cordones por supuestos."* (My shoestrings of course.) Soaking my feet in a Costa Rica jail's contaminated floor water wasn't exactly something I had in mind.

My Air Force sneakers were one of the last personal possessions I had retained after being robbed at least twice. After the third month of selling what had been left in the restaurant, I was defunct of sellable products to help me eat. Every sunrise after sleeping in my disease-ridden restaurant had been like pulling a one-armed bandit in a casino, hoping a loan, donation, or friendly offer would put food on my plate.

I carefully untied my sneaker strings in a dry area of my new home's bio floor and handed them to the waiting officer.

"¿Por que pegaste la mujer?" (Why did you hit the woman?), he asked condescendingly.

The officer automatically assumed that I'd hit the woman who'd put me in jail. I was initially shocked that he had insulted me, but while I was collecting my breath, I came to the realization that physical abuse could be something that was common in gringo relationships with the women of Costa Rica. After being in Costa Rica for fifteen years, nothing surprised me. I understood that in my position as a gringo at the mercy of the Costa Rican guard, it was in my best interest to remain calm. *"Yo nunca le pegaría a una mujer"* (I never hit women), I replied.

Clank, click, click. The officer closed the door and locked it.

I scanned my cell thoroughly. I never thought my life would be on the line in more ways than one. The first thing to do was look for the least contaminated location in which to park myself. I was in shock and in self-preservation high alert. I observed every inch of the jail floor. The dry level was to the far left. The only place to sit was on a concrete slab that lined the back wall of the cell. There was a combination of unidentified objects in the puddles leading to the concrete slab. The object that stood out the most was positioned on the floor in the far-left corner just below the slab. I focused on the twin bloody cotton swabs as I tiptoed my way over to my new bed. Desperation and disease occupied my thoughts. When I got closer to my bed, I was disgusted to see the raindrops of dried blood that decorated two-thirds of my concrete mattress. The most inviting area of my bed was at the far left. There was just enough room to sit. That was all I planned to do.

I should have been grateful. They could have given me the junior suite. It came with double concrete slabs, graffiti-decorated walls, and a completely contaminated floor. I decided to do some reading as I scanned the graffiti in the neighboring cell. There were various items that weren't very entertaining.

As I moved my eyes to the right, I noticed two names in large letters. The first one was "CHINO." It interested me, but I wasn't surprised. "Chino" was the ex-mayor of the beach town in which I had resided. What really took me off guard was the next name in large letters: TONY. Now that just wasn't cool. Did someone have a premonition that I or all *Tonys* were going to end up in this Costa Rica jail? *Oh Yes! My Costa Rican dream: paradise, piña coladas, Coronas, Bob Marley, long semi-romantic walks on the beach to watch the sun set into the Pacific Ocean, and Tony in a jail with his name on the wall like an Expedia reservation.*

When I was living in the abandoned restaurant, I had no resources at all. I had to worry every day if I would get one meal. My skin was turning hard and black from the unsanitary conditions I had been living in. During this time, my wife had taken my daughter to live with her mother in Panama. My son's mother, who'd put me in jail, had a very experienced Tico lawyer who must have informed my ex-fiancé that I was now worth much more dead than alive.

I had dug and scratched my way out of the ghetto, entered the world of the richest people on earth, and lived the dreams of the majority. I was now five thousand miles from home, regressing to my personal Central American ghetto. My fatherless decisions had finally caught up to me. I thought I had it all under control. All my life, golden doors had opened in time to solve life's problems. The doors were no longer there. I had used my very generous allotment. My arrogance made my spiritual guide's pause.

The nightmare enhanced when the dusk mosquitoes invited their friends and family into my cell to feast on my already infected blood. They weren't very picky. Some mosquitoes carried dengue. You can be infected with dengue once, but you'd better be in very good health if you get it twice.

I sat up straight in my very limited space, crossed my arms and legs, and prepared my mind to be an all-night washing machine of my invasive criminal thoughts of revenge. My fight against the mosquito clouds and for my life commenced.

Chapter 1

THE CANDLELIGHT DANCED SOLO IN THE CORNER OF THE EMPTY BAR, trying to calm my hunger, frustration, and anger. I double-checked the usual signs indicating the coast was clear from the clouds of satisfied mosquitos that finished their nightly feast of my blood. My pen, the only companion and confidant I had left, desperately clung to my hand while I lowered it to the waiting pad of paper. It was time to tell my story; it was time to save my life.

I was an African American ghetto kid, raised in 1960s Boston, Massachusetts. Most of us didn't know how poor we were. Our single mothers would sacrifice everything necessary to make us think everything was all right. The kids would play, practicing to be players, hookers, drug dealers, or thieves. Some of us were talented enough to become professional athletes.

It was commonplace to hear drunks singing in the street, and no one was surprised to see dead bodies in the street either. Violence was a national ghetto pastime—bullets or fists were always flying through the air somewhere. At one point during our adolescence, my brother and I had been playing basketball with a local gang leader and his brother. When my brother challenged a foul the gang leader called on me, he pulled his gun, held it to my brother's head, and asked him to reconsider.

The ghetto had fringe benefits designed to keep its inhabitants in their containment area. Young girls would have babies at a rapid pace and receive welfare benefits and food stamps. A lot of the babies would eventually be taken care of by their grandmothers, who would also share the increased amounts of food stamps and welfare checks. The misery of the babies and their broke, escapist fathers created a tribe of insecure young mothers who effectively dulled their rejections with an abundance of alcohol and drugs.

My father left my mother with four boys and one girl when I was only one year old, leaving her consistently stressed and angry with life. My older siblings and I grew up in a constant state of never knowing when Mom would take out her frustrations on us. She started her religious journey in the Baptist Church around the time I began elementary school. She became so deeply engrossed in her newfound faith that she got the spirit one day and almost fell off the balcony where she had been singing with the choir. When she converted to the Jehovah's Witnesses right before my eleventh Christmas—and I did not see a tree or presents in the morning—I truly felt we had lost each other to religion.

My sister, Sheila, was the oldest; she was beautiful, smart, athletic, and tough. Sheila would eventually succumb to the attraction of men and the feel-good candies of the streets. Richard was next in line; we'd lost his twin when they were five years old. Richard was very athletic and spent many hours playing sports before his frustrations led him into his own string of bad luck. Oscar stood in the middle of the boys. He was named after my father, for a good reason; he emulated our father—he was the perfect clone. I was the baby, so I had a front-row seat to my siblings' theater. I must have slept through some scenes because I would go on to repeat some of their mistakes.

My father was a truck-driving macho man from Atlanta, Georgia; he was admired by many men for how he used his good looks and charisma to manipulate situations and women. My siblings and I would worship him as a god during the very few times he would visit. I knew my father was highly respected on the streets, but I didn't know how dangerous he could be until I was in my teenage years. He shot a man to death for threatening to blow up his house.

My saving grace was a white family who appeared almost out of nowhere. They embraced me and opened the world up to me so that when I had to make a decision, I had a chance to make the right choice. The Torreys were teachers at the Mount Hermon Preparatory School in Northfield. They had reached out to the local Catholic priest of my community to seek connections with some nice colored kids to integrate with their children because they did not want to raise their kids in an all-white environment. The priest connected my sister and me with the Torreys; my sister did not get along with some of them, but I had a lot of fun with the Torreys. After one visit with the Torreys, I fell in love with them—and they fell in love with me. I found myself staying with them on almost every vacation. I learned and did wonderful things with them on the outside of the ghetto world.

I was lucky to have this wild-card family. They made me want to have more than the norm in my life and pushed me to excel academically. I was always in the advanced classes at my elementary school. I even won the Boston mayor's award for academics at the end of my sixth-grade year. I was prepared to follow my peers to the public Lewis Junior High school. Little did I know that my mother was plotting with the Torreys to put me on an academic and cultural rocket ship.

I didn't go to the Lewis School. The prescribed pattern for my life seemed to undergo a mutation. I spent three years, 1970–73, at a very happy private middle school called Shady Hill in Cambridge, Massachusetts. Most of the kids at Shady Hill had started prep school education at prekindergarten. From the well-educated parents and teachers to the students, I could tell that the majority of my peers were very intelligent. I felt I had been flipped upside down as soon as I entered my homeroom. The teacher and the students gave me a warm welcome, but I knew I had a lot to learn to survive mentally in my new atmosphere.

By the grace of the gods and Mr. Torrey, I was accepted into a very prestigious prep high school, Loomis-Chaffee, in Windsor, Connecticut. I was placed into dorms with kids who seemed to be some of the most interesting international adolescents on this earth. Trying to study, socialize, and become a marijuana connoisseur at the same time was quite the challenge. By the time I enrolled at the University of Massachusetts, I had evolved into a wild and hormonal "Black preppy jumping bean," with my wild partying and fast lifestyle.

The boarding school had strict guidelines about the times you could eat, sleep, and leave the campus. UMass was wide-open. I called my own shots. Math was my strength. I passed everything up to Calculus 1. I thought an engineering major would be a breeze. I signed up for Calculus 2, Fortran, and a couple of other courses I thought I could party through. I had no guidance whatsoever; if I did, it was hidden deep inside my subconscious.

My college years danced to the beat of many different drummers. Outside, I was black; inside, I was a confused and extremely selfish chameleon. By the time I arrived at UMass, I was culturally diverse and comfortable with the underpinnings of almost every social level in American society. I was able to adjust my movements and phonetics to connect with everyone—from people in the ghetto to people wearing Brooks Brothers blazers. However, my chameleon bag of tricks didn't count much with students who insisted upon separating themselves from any culture outside of their own.

Individuality and insecurity prevented me from joining any campus groups. I spent minimal time with any of them, including the black students' groups. I felt support groups would suppress me from using my full social capacity, smothering me into their own brands and dulling my chameleon-like capabilities. I followed my own path.

I may not have had a great academic career, but I brought athletic talent. Seeing my abilities, the varsity lacrosse coach at UMass tried everything he could to keep me on his team during my first year. However, 90 percent of my teammates wanted to make me disappear. My attendance was horrendous. Most of my teammates were from Long Island, which produced some of the best lacrosse players in the world. The combination of their close community, above-average income level, and a very high winning percentage made the lacrosse players very popular throughout the UMass community. The players, including the fringed outcasts among them, were automatically invited to the majority of campus parties. The free kegs and pretty girls fit right into my almost nonexistent class schedule.

My chameleon presentations did not sit well with my teammates. I was sent a direct signal from them during an inter-squad scrimmage. I made a solid but legal hit on one of the more popular teammates. Instead of the "Great hit!" usually awarded to the other teammates, I heard, "Get the fuck up off of him!"

The varsity coach knew I was talented enough to be on the team, but my presence assured that he had his work cut out for him socially and politically. His weight was lifted at the end of the fall of my freshman year when I made the mistake of using a new, hard lacrosse stick at the last preseason scrimmage. I was in the open. The midfielder threw me the ball for a very high-percentage goal. When the ball hit my new stick, it reacted like most balls when they hit a lacrosse stick that is not broken in; it bounced right out. The opposing team's defense had enough time to get into position. I looked like I had never played the game. I wasn't very surprised when my name wasn't on the roster the next day. I played junior varsity through the spring season.

I had missed the basketball tryouts, but I decided to try to get on the basketball team at UMass that year when the lacrosse season ended. I showed up for the varsity practice and was sent directly to the junior varsity coach. The coach could either see that I had potential, or he remembered that I'd scored twenty points when my high school had played against his team the previous season. That poor JV coach had no idea who he was dealing with when he decided to sign me on.

I'd had a very bad experience during my senior year of high school with my varsity basketball coach. I'd missed practice once, opting to get my buzz on instead, because my back was hurting. When I returned the next day, one of my teammates was angry at me for skipping, and he physically aggressed me. This was a serious offense as far as the school was concerned and they were planning on throwing this other player out of the athletic program under which he had been admitted. The coach wanted him on the team, so he decided to pay me a surprise visit at my dorm room to ask me to vouch for this player to the disciplinary board. When he dropped in, I had two girls and a bong in my dorm room. I ended up taking a bribe from the coach: he now had information that could get me expelled, so I agreed to testify on his other players' behalf on the condition that he would not get me expelled from the school for the weed and the girls, whom he'd found hiding in my closet during his surprise visit. Retaining my spot on the team was not part of the agreement; I was off.

Did I bring a negative attitude to basketball at UMass? Of course! The majority of people from my neighborhood were born with attitudes. The experience I'd had in high school had only added fuel.

It only took sitting this ten-year starter on the bench for the entire first game of the season to find out what kind of attitude I actually had. You know you have the gift of gab—or a shit attitude—when you can rip into your leader, make three-quarters of the team quit, lose a buddy for life, and put the lights out on UMass JV basketball for the rest of the season. Needless to say, I did not play basketball at UMass after that.

How the hell did I get so spoiled without a dollar in hand? The private schools tried to refine my attitude, but I still had a lot of anger in me I couldn't fully evaluate. My friends, family, and I had to respond to any and all threats in the ghetto. It takes time and a lot of self-evaluation to not stick out your chest and to lower the hair on your back. When you're from the ghetto, you don't have a chip on your shoulder; you have a log. I just pity the fool who pisses off a young ghetto man who spent thousands of prep school hours absorbing the minds of the future "masters of the universe."

Midway through my junior year at UMass, I realized I was on the fast track to nowhere. I turned in my registration paperwork late. At that point in my life, I was in a completely different world than my mother, who, like most parents in my neighborhood, had no knowledge of college administrative processes. I was never reminded, pushed, or advised to do anything at this point. Since the seventh grade, I had been on my own to learn how to be responsible with school. The university supplied me with a dorm room but no meal plan.

I took out a $1,500 student loan, which filled the gas tank of my relationship with my new girlfriend, and we enjoyed a three-week supply of pizza and beer to replace our well-spent calories. I eventually worked my way into a very low-paying dorm-monitoring job. The job, well below minimum wage, filled my stomach twice a day with peanut butter and jelly sandwiches. An old friend from Shady Hill would spoil me with a hamburger once a week. The writing was clear and precise on the wall: I was done. I called my very disappointed mother and cried like a baby. I decided I would at least do the best I could to maintain a 2.0 to keep the UMass doors open.

In the "care package students'" worlds, Mom and Dad would get on the phone, coach their child through some adjustments, give positive reinforcement, and send some extra cash; that world wasn't mine. I was tired of being poor. Reruns of an image in my mind starring an ignorant white guy who'd been expelled for hate crimes returning to visit friends in a brand-new car dominated my brain. I thought, *If an asshole like him can go out into the world and return to campus in a shiny new car, it should be a slam dunk for me.*

I pulled my academic socks up and secured a 2.0 overall grade average. To this very day, I wonder if I missed my calling; I received an "AB" in Physics. Even though I had kept the door open to remain at UMass if I wanted to, I decided of my own accord to drop out.

I packed my bags; this broken-family, undisciplined, under-skilled, without-a-clue young ghetto kid walked ass-backwards into his quest to conquer the world.

I began my dropout career by bouncing drunks out of bars, bartending, and selling encyclopedias door-to-door in the dead of winter. I had the perfect directions to run straight into a brick wall.

I was job shopping with my morning coffee when I came across an announcement from the Benjamin Franklin Institute of Technology. They were offering a government-sponsored course for computer electronics and technology with a grant they had received from President Reagan's inner-city development program. The program paid qualified participants a hundred dollars per week to help them with their living expenses. The course was not your typical class; the classes were held for one year, eight hours a day, five days a week. There were no breaks for the entire year. The college-accredited courses consisted of math, English, and afternoon computer labs. The students would build a basic personal computer motherboard from scratch.

I could not have applied at a faster pace. My income easily fit under the maximum requirements in order to be eligible for the program; this enlightened encyclopedia salesman knew this opportunity could be one of his last chances to achieve the kind of life he wanted.

A year later, I graduated in the top 5 percent of my computer electronics class. As part of the program, representatives from IBM and Wang were to come to the Benjamin Franklin Institute to address our class and conduct job interviews. The representative from Wang never showed.

The IBM human resource manager came the following day. He spoke to the entire class for about half an hour and left without conducting any interviews. I was standing by his car by the time he got to it on his way out. He handed me his card and said, "You are the kind of person we are looking for." I followed up, landed an interview, passed my entrance exam, and began my first "real job" with what was at the time one of the top corporations on earth.

Chapter 2

LIFE WAS MOVING IN THE RIGHT DIRECTION. I HAD A GREAT JOB, A SOLID roommate, a nice girlfriend, and money in the bank, and I was bartending for extra money at night.

The Father's Corporation owned a collection of bars around the greater Boston area. They were sleazy English pubs frequented by bikers and white borderline AA-bound college students. After working a day at IBM, I would head to the Harvard Square Father's bar, "The Bow and Arrow," for my shift. I lived near Father's First, which was open until two o'clock in the morning. The Bow and Arrow closed at one, so after work, I would jump into my car and race to Father's First for a nightcap.

One special night, my blond "player" friend joined me for my usual nightcap. He saw a cute woman on the other side of the bar and became determined to add her to his list of accomplishments. I'd had a full day and just assumed he would leave with this woman. I looked up after a few minutes to watch him work his magic and was absolutely amazed to see this very cute curly-haired woman making him feel a lot shorter than he already was. When my friend crawled back in humiliation to his seat beside me, I looked across the bar at this very impressive woman, and another extremely unlikely mutation of my life's pattern began. I didn't know it at the time, but I was looking into the eyes of the future Mrs. Anthony Florence.

She was looking at me directly in the eye and smiling. I smiled back, but I did not approach her for fear of being torn into the way she had done with my friend. She was waiting for me at the door as I left and did not hesitate when I asked if I could drive her home. The attraction between us was magnetic and inevitable. That night was the night I began to finally understand the concept of "soul mates." Joanna was wild, kinetic, and adorably pretty. No matter how many times her friends tried to separate us that night, it was impossible. We simply connected; we wouldn't disconnect for the next twenty-two years.

Our relationship, almost from the start, was anything but stable and functional. At some point, I was able to tell that there was something wrong, but I kept pushing it out of my mind. Was it that Joanna felt she needed to hunt down some white powder before we spent our first night together? Or was it that after I helped her pay the four hundred dollars to remove the traffic boot from her car, she spontaneously decided to back her car into mine? Maybe it was that during our romantic trip to Cape Cod, she threw her drink on me because I'd taken too much time in the bathroom? It's amazing how strong infatuation is; any one of those events should have been a clear signal of a dysfunctional relationship.

One night, I was sitting in Father's First, and one of her closest male friends decided to inform me that I was not only getting a good-looking girl; I was getting the daughter of "The Chairman." This upgraded ghetto kid already had his brain on overload just with everything that had happened to him in the past ten years. I had no extra time to be a "wannabe" and search out who was who in the stratosphere of business or finances. I had no idea what company Joanna's friend was talking about. I just assumed that her father had an office at an expensive New York address. I guess Joanna had tried to send me a signal when she bought me a five-hundred-dollar leather jacket with a check that bounced to Mars, showing me that she knew how to act rich—even when she didn't have the funds to back it up. (The funds would always eventually come; her family dispensed her trust fund to her at their discretion). The store owner must have seen something in her; he would have never accepted that size check from me.

Joanna and I connected on many different levels; our souls were definitely meant to connect for our spiritual growth. I cut ties with my other girlfriend and moved in with Joanna at her Allston, Massachusetts, apartment less than a month after we began dating. As I was walking up to her apartment with my things, I passed her ex on his way out with his things.

I continued to work both jobs. Joanna would wait for me at Bow and Arrow and drink an abundance of employee-discount drinks until I'd eventually join her at the end of the night.

I made it to work every single day, although many days I would be a little fuzzy headed with a high probability of smelling like a stale cocktail. I was young enough to shake it off within a couple of hours. It was great that I was a field service engineer, making calls to customers to repair small computers, typewriters, and copiers. As long as I hustled, I could distribute my time between customer visits and resting at home to make up for the minimum amounts of sleep Joanna and I got during the night.

Our relationship continued to bond us deeper into a fatal attraction. Given the fact that our puberty years were spent within the same type of social academic cultures, we had enough in common to draw each other in like magnets. Joanna, like me, had attended private and boarding schools for most of her life, and like me, she had been a rebel who smoked weed in her dorms and experimented with psychedelics. We both went straight to cocktails after work. Joanna was brought up by a Swedish nanny and had started hitting the liquor cabinet at the tender age of seven. I, too, had been on my own as I forged my way through certain other very mature rites of passage at the delicate age of eleven.

When I was in boarding school, I was very comfortable with the fact that, when school was in session, the students were at the same social level, no matter how the finances were distributed. However, this was not the case in our relationship; Joanna, like most of my former private school peers, had a huge financial advantage over me and loved to tout it over my head.

Joanna was a hard-rock, heavy-drinking, Camel-non-filter-smoking seventies hippie wild child. Children saw a very attractive side of her; she had a big heart that extended warm energy that young children were drawn to. My mother, however, was not a child. She was very disappointed when her son brought home this neglected "white trash" with holes in her jeans and sweaters into her home.

Joanna had about as much interest in filtering her actions as she did her cigarettes. I am sure that when she was young and her parents would leave for their offshore businesses and lovers, the Swedish nanny would try to rid the world of the evil child by sucking her up into the vacuum cleaner because Joanna really knew how to get a person angry.

I was so stimulated by this pretty and wild woman that I tolerated all the visits by her various personalities. Her main alternate personality was "Katherine." Joanna's mother had named the personality after a character in *Wuthering Heights*. Katherine would possess Joanna to protect her after she had a certain number of drinks. Katherine, to put it mildly, was the bitch from hell. Katherine would appear, verbally target you, skipping over the demonic Latin and using the Queen's English to make sure you understood every word while she tore you a new asshole. Katherine made sure Joanna passed out just before we had time to exorcise her. Don't get me completely wrong; sometimes Katherine could work in your favor, especially in the bedroom.

While Joanna and I were living together, she was forced by her parents to fly to New York and have dinner with young men from the right families. Planned marriages are still alive and well in blue-blood America. I was not ecstatic about the slaps in the face, but Joanna always assured me that she had no interest in the guy's her parents were trying to align her with.

The caste system dates came to an abrupt end when Katherine decided enough was enough. Joanna's date probably said something that woke Katherine early, which led to both personalities working together to literally break her date's nose at a very expensive restaurant. The phone rang as soon as Joanna arrived home. Howard was on the line. He rarely called. Joanna was always very uncomfortable communicating with her father. To our understandably great shock and relief, he was calling to invite us both out to dinner, asking her to have me choose the restaurant.

It was only the second time I had been formally invited to have dinner with a white girlfriend's parents. The first time had been when I was attending my private junior high school. Marrika was very pretty and lived in a single-parent home like I did. Her mother was a conservative librarian who rarely smiled, yet she tolerated this young man who was very obviously not trying to *study* with her daughter. Marrika and I would spend many hours alone in her basement kissing. I think she had made an abstinence deal with her mother because it was enforced every single time.

I chose the North End steakhouse, a place a private school classmate's father had once taken us before a Boston Celtics basketball game. Joanna's parents flew in that weekend. Her father asked many career- and business-oriented questions that kept me on my toes. Her mother, on the other hand, was very pleasant toward me.

I passed the initial test. It was the first time I'd had to use the dinner table aesthetics my prep school had taught me, instinctively matching my forks, knives, and spoons to specific plates.

Invitations to New York City ignited. Joanna's mother had a new hobby of presenting to her circle the young "black sheep" who'd stolen the family rebel's heart. Joanna was always flown in early on these trips to get some private time with her family before I would join. She was required to give them the lowdown she couldn't discuss in front of me, including why I still wore polyester.

On the first of these trips, I remember nervously shifting and pretending to read the airport magazines, doing everything not to giggle as the economy-class passengers passed my first-class seat. The stewardess took some of the pressure off when she handed me my mimosa. It was a very short and extremely comfortable flight to New York City.

The chauffeur was attentively waiting when I arrived outside the baggage claim. He was very professional and dying to meet the young man of his race who had more than one foot in his boss's private door. The chauffeur's trademark champagne greeting was followed by a Brooks Brothers box. I opened the box to find the perfect-sized dark blue blazer. I had another prep school flashback as I admired my first blazer. I had a vivid memory of my private institution peers relentlessly wearing these blue blazers during parental visits and graduations.

We drove directly to Manhattan and stopped in front of a restaurant called "The Russian Tea Room." Joanna's father, mother, and stepfather were anxiously awaiting my arrival. Joanna's stepfather, Morton, was her mother's first husband and the father of the three oldest of her mother's five female children. Morton was the poster boy of refinement. His tailors probably wanted to commit suicide every time he walked through their door. I don't think he ever approved of me. It would have been nice, but I eventually learned to live with his lack of approval.

I tried to keep up with all the nuances that were tied to actually participating in the lives of this foreign culture. I was impressed but not surprised at how Joanna handled every privileged detail with ease. She had begun learning what one needed to know before leaving the birth canal. I, on the other hand, felt like I was attending a crash course in social-elite rocket science. Even though we were indulged with the best of the best on those trips, we were extremely relieved to leave the refined stress cloud that came with that territory and return to our smog when our plane landed back home in Boston.

No one ever worried about Joanna getting pregnant; she had explained how she never used birth control because her family's doctor said she was barren. Being a macho man, my first thought had been: *Exactly how many times did she not have to use birth control?* The second thought had followed with: *No wonder her parents aren't too concerned about our relationship; they have a "get out of jail free" card!*

Joanna and I persisted through all the quests we deemed necessary to validate our relationship. Destiny was more powerful than I could have ever imagined. I finally squeezed out of our party money the three hundred dollars needed to buy the engagement ring she'd chosen. A decent bottle of champagne next to one candle was the best presentation I could assemble for my first marriage proposal.

We decided to celebrate by joining her envious guy friend Mike at a Kentucky Derby party at his aunt's house in Washington, DC. A fun drive gradually developed into a nightmare, beginning when Mike explained to the officer who'd pulled him over for speeding that he didn't have a license. The DC trip continued its path to complete destruction when, after the party and our following barhopping, we incurred two traffic tickets on our way back to the hotel and crashed the car, rendering it almost undrivable. I woke up the next morning absolutely shocked to see a third ticket for running a red light that I absolutely did not remember. We were getting more proficient at fucking up.

A couple of weeks after the initial DC trip, I headed back out there to check on the car, which we'd left at a repair shop.

As soon as I returned home, Joanna had an announcement for me. "I'm pregnant!" Joanna's aura could not contain the glow that exploded across her face like a tsunami wave. I think it would definitely be an understatement to say that I was a bit taken aback. I'm sure the doctor who told her that she could not have children was not the cheapest doctor in Manhattan. As a matter of fact, when it comes to such the delicate task of informing one that their Jewish-American princesses couldn't give them grandchildren, you would think an extremely rich, generous, and relationship-based woman such as Joanna's mother would make sure it was carried out by one of the best doctors on this earth.

My new fiancée and I were now working, partying, and paying for a rental car. Always broke, we were engaged to be married and pregnant. What a wonderful start.

The week following Joanna's announcement, a friend and I were at a bar together. The car repair place in DC was not communicating well with me about whether or not our car was ready, so I decided to pay them another visit. Since my friend wanted to visit his girlfriend in Connecticut, we decided to head south together after the bar closed. How and when we arrived at his beautiful girlfriend's Ocean Cove Greenwich mansion will continue to be a mystery. I was directed to one of the guest rooms to recover.

Later that night, I received a call from a very distraught Joanna. I'd never felt so helpless in my life. Joanna's pain exuded through the telephone. She had been racked with agony, crying and bleeding all night. Joanna explained how a small figure had fallen out of her body when she'd gone to the toilet. I couldn't imagine how horrified she must have been, watching the child she would never know fall bleeding and dead from her barren womb. I was six hundred miles away; I couldn't be there to comfort my future wife. I had to listen over the phone while Joanna was having one of the worst times of her life. I returned from my excursion without my car, and the knife completed its depth when Joanna informed me that her ex-boyfriend had come to our apartment to treat her to Chinese food.

You can't party into a relationship of trust. We were not spiritually stable, so how the hell could we be there for each other? We were in our early twenties, and our brains were programmed to not give a shit in order to maintain human population levels.

Within sixty party days, Joanna was pregnant again. This time, it lasted the term. A mental and physical base was put under our relationship; we went from being a couple to a family. Our lives seemed to upgrade overnight; Joanna's family began to take better financial care of us. The wedding date was moved up by six months to beat the baby bump. It got a little uncomfortable when Joanna's best friend decided to update Joanna's mother about the fact that my father was a murderer a day before the wedding. It made me a lot more interesting of an in-law, but Joanna had some explaining to do. My future mother-in-law eventually calmed, knowing that my father had left me when I was only one year old, giving him minimum time to educate me on how to conduct myself. The wedding was on.

Howard's estate garden was the perfect place to celebrate the fusion of two distinct social economic cultures. The wedding took place at the end of November, and there were space heaters everywhere. Joanna was the only person out of more than two hundred attendees to get close enough to a space heater to catch her dress on fire. My mother, who now understood that a hole in a cashmere sweater was preppy teenage fashion, put out the fire without thinking about her own safety. I was now officially part of Howard's family.

Joanna's mother's entourage in attendance at our wedding included the likes of Bart Howard ("Fly me to the Moon"), Benny Goodman ("King of Swing"), the family who owned the Empire State Building, all of my new wife's rich ex-boyfriends, and an assortment of extremely famous interior designers. My family was there to fill my half of the very mixed cultural bowl. Our wedding was the Olympics of gossip and alcohol.

Chapter 3

OUR BEAUTIFUL BABY GIRL, ANTONIA, WAS BORN THE FOLLOWING MAY. Joanna had completely straightened up during her pregnancy; she'd stopped smoking and drinking, except for an occasional doctor-approved glass of port wine. I, being the child of a "Papa was a rolling stone," resisted change. I was very uncomfortable with anything that formed outside of my schematics.

I tried to be on my best behavior whenever we visited Joanna's parents. It was not easy to converse with Howard about anything but high finances. I wondered if there was any warm blood hidden somewhere deep inside of him. One thing Howard once told me that would forever stick out in my memory was: "Make sure you have done your homework."

There is one particular visit that will stick with me to the grave. Almost a couple of years into the marriage, I decided to have a conversation with him while he was tending to one of his *Architectural Digest*-worthy gardens. I started talking to him about everything that he wasn't interested in: family, cars, or his daughter. In the middle of the conversation, he stopped gardening, his clear blue eyes looked directly into mine, and he calmly said, "You are very lucky."

Most straight shooters were either survivors or victims in the ghetto. We liked throwing curves, not fastballs. Howard threw me a thousand-mile-per-hour mental fastball, and all I could do was put a stupid smile on my face. This self-made IBM customer engineer was a little bit insulted. I looked around at his pristine estate, which consisted of two medium-sized houses, two guest cottages, and a swimming pool surrounded by beautiful gardens. I figured he had a couple million. I thought, *Maybe I'm not in his position, but I can get there. I made my way out of the ghetto, I have a good job, and time is on my side. I am a success story from where I come from!* I made an excuse to walk away so I could clear my head. The log on my shoulder vibrated, practically breaking my shoulder bone. In my mind, I said, *Howard, your daughter is lucky.*

How wrong was I? I was about to get my first wake-up call with regard to my assumptions. I needed a lot more "wannabe" training than I'd gotten in prep school. It seemed I had married into the Howard family right before he completely came out of his financial closet. Two years after I joined his family, Howard started to really enjoy the fruits of his labor. I found myself vacationing in one of the family's three (new?) South Hampton, New York, beachfront mansions. As it turned out, I may, in fact, have been the lucky one. We spent most of our vacation time with my easygoing mother-in-law. She enjoyed the entertainment provided by my edgy personality and maverick tendencies, courtesy of my background on the other side of the socioeconomic divide.

Chapter 4

IT WAS AMAZING HOW POWERFUL JOANNA'S PERSUASIONS COULD BE when she was under the influence of her mother. We were only in the middle of the lease on our Allston apartment when our first child was born, and the decision was made—not by me—for my new family to relocate to New York. It only took one week of Joanna forcefully throwing mental and physical hints at me for me to find myself literally driving the wrong way on a very familiar one-way street near our apartment one night on my way home because of how stressed I was. It was a wake-up call that I could not fight Joanna's will; her baby needed to be close to her family.

We packed up and headed to New York. The easiest part of making the trip was comfortably driving our U-Haul into Joanna's parents' Westchester County estate parking lot; we weren't imposing, as there was room for ten more vehicles.

I was in good standing with IBM. My manager, Paul, was good to me and made arrangements for me to transfer to the Harrison, New York, field service location. Joanna's parents gave "our" decision to move a safety net. They let us live in one of the houses on the estate until we found a place closer to my office. The New York elite comfort packages seemed to show up even before we knew we needed them.

Chapter 5

THE WHITE PLAINS IBM SALES MANAGER HEARD ABOUT ME AS THE customer engineer who was winning every sales-lead contest. One day as I walked by his office, he called me by name and signaled with his pointer finger for me to come inside of his office. "Hello Tony," he said fondly, his head to the side as he looked at me with a half-smile.

I, on the other hand, entered his office with a large and enthusiastic smile. He knew my name and I had never formally met him!

"You want to sell, don't you?" the manager asked, his head continuing to bop up and down.

"Of course!" I responded confidently. He pulled out the paperwork and started the process of promoting me to salesman right away.

To prepare for the entrance exam to the sales job, I had to buy an algebra book and study it much more in-depth than I had ever done in high school. The IBM sales entrance exam was more than math and English; one wouldn't have been able to prepare for all of it using external study materials. Most of the answers had to be naturally implanted in your brain, a part of your personality.

I was getting pretty cocky with my new position on the social ladder. Rather than keeping my secrets from envy, I had openly shared my personal information and success story with my colleagues. I had to hang my technical manager at the Harrison field service location out to dry when he tried to block me from joining the IBM sales force by not giving me ample time to study for the entrance exam. I went over his head, making a stink to his boss and scoring the opportunity to take a second test with enough time to study.

Chapter 6

THE IBM SALES "BOOT CAMP" WAS HELD IN ATLANTA, GEORGIA. THE training lasted for about a year, with six weeks to be completed in Atlanta and six to be completed at my new home IBM location in White Plains, New York. It was an intense pressure chamber. Most of the students were recruited from the top of the graduating classes at their respective universities. They came with fancy degrees and awards; I came with baggage and insecurity. Most students would attend after-class study groups; I enjoyed martinis at a local club. My manager knew my potential, but I had to continuously fight his manager to keep me in the class. My IBM career hit a fine line when I came to class late and ruffled from a lack of sleep. My manager's manager called me into his office and read me the riot act. Studying from my home location in White Plains was more comfortable since I had a plethora of support there.

My home life grew more complicated as the trust factor in my marriage fell to an all-time low. I admitted to a one-night stand I'd had with a girl I'd met at a club one night in Atlanta, and Joanna hinted about having an affair as well. We were on the fast track to destruction, but we pretended we were building force fields around us with extra cocktails. I made a rule for myself to not drink during business hours, but Joanna had no alcohol restrictions. She worked out of the house or hung out with a male drinking buddy at their real estate office.

Through the thickening fog of our drinking and marriage problems, I tried to keep my eye on the ball at work. I straightened up at IBM's boot camp and decided to prove why my manager had sent me there. I rose to the top of my class and received IBM sales and marketing awards. I proudly graduated from the training as a high-potential sales executive.

Two months after my sales training, my personal computer IBM division was sold to New York New England Telephone (NYNEX). IBM followed their old culture of employee protection by offering me a position in their mainframe division. I was still fresh into the personal computer division, and Joanna and I were still overspending. It wasn't a very difficult decision for me to take the five thousand dollars NYNEX offered me to cross over to their company.

NYNEX business centers were very comfortable places to do business. They tried, but they were not able to maintain the same level of status as IBM. Computer architecture and marketing became a playground for start-up companies such as Compaq, Apple, and Leading Edge. The competition gained a healthy percentage of the personal computer market share at a rapid pace.

I became one of the top ten sales representatives in the company and had the responsibility of stepping up as interim manager from time to time at the White Plains office, which was constantly rotating managers. I eventually began seeking managerial positions elsewhere. I was looking to advance my career, figuring that if I could be an interim manager at NYNEX, I could be a manager somewhere else. I was offered a branch manager job at Computer Factory, a competing company. They didn't have very much financial muscle, but they were very aggressive. I was able to grow into a national marketing manager's job within a couple short years.

A couple years after I joined Computer Factory, a more successful PC retailer purchased the company and liquidated absolutely everyone and everything. I got a national sales manager job with a small startup company and eventually got noticed by Philips Electronics, and they hired me to be their Northeast Regional Sales Manager.

During my growth spurt, I almost made enough money to support my family's out-of-control spending. Joanna's family packages included full tuition for our daughter's very expensive private school, 50 percent discounts on exotic travel vacation packages, and healthy birthday and Christmas checks. We would max out our credit cards every year enjoying fine food and exotic vacations. My family traveled first-class to places such as Sweden, France, Spain, Morocco, Egypt, Tanzania, Israel, Turkey, Cyprus, and Mexico.

As the Northeast Regional Sales Manager at Philips, it was my job to get product to our dealers, who then sold it to consumers. I developed a relationship with one of the guys in our dealer network, a Panamanian man named Alberto. Alberto had just been hired at one of our dealer locations in New Jersey. I could tell he had a hunger to succeed, and I wanted to help him. I began attending sales calls with him, teaching him everything

I knew about closing sales. I didn't know it when I met him, but eventually he told me he had been involved in a murder trial and had done time. He eventually turned out to be one of the top salespersons in the professional video products industry.

I couldn't help but be impressed with how he often used Spanish to charm many Latina secretaries who were effectively the corporate doorkeepers and could either grant or block our access as salesmen to our potential corporate clients. I began to see the ability to speak and understand Spanish as being an advantage in the business world. Thus, Joanna and I decided that it would be a good idea to immerse our daughter, who was now in her early teenage years, in Spanish. For two consecutive summer vacations, we sent her to Latin countries to stay with non-English speaking families, the first visit being in Costa Rica, and the second in Uruguay.

Chapter 7

SEVENTEEN YEARS OF DYSFUNCTIONAL BLISS CAN DO A LOT OF DAMAGE to two very stubborn people. Fine foods, vacations, cocktails, and continuously trying to pay completely unnecessary expenditures were starting to take their toll on my marriage. I tried to convince myself that I was focused and belittle my personal donations to my family's imbalances. When I wasn't on one of my very frequent road trips, I would lock myself in my home office until "happy hour."

Ghetto families love, just like all the other families on earth. The survival pressures of some ghetto families will turn each member into a bloodsucking eel when one of their children or siblings not only melts into white people's walls, but actually obtains a legal address of success.

Thanks to the eighties' introduction of crack, all my siblings fell into an almost unavoidable trap of addiction to this very inexpensive poison. I felt, and Joanna agreed, we needed to share the blessing the Torrey family had given me and give something back to my family. I wanted to open the eyes of the children of my siblings. Joanna was a natural-born socialite, and she fell right into the idea of a camp to enlighten our deprived nephews and nieces. "Camp Florence" was born.

We had a pool and a forest for all the kids to enjoy. Absolutely everyone had a great time during our family's camp. I would lecture all the kids against drugs and teach every five-year-old how to swim. Joanna cooked and hugged. There was excessive drinking among the adults and continuous dancing. One thing my family loved to do was dance, and there wasn't one minute without it.

I think we went a little too far when we also allowed my nieces' and nephews' addicted parents to spread their rehabilitation sounds, smells, and juices around our daughter during off-camp seasons.

Chapter 8

I HAD BECOME A VERY SUCCESSFUL MANAGER WITH AN IMPRESSIVE market share increase, and my customers were very comfortable doing business with me. For the first time in my career, I felt content.

However, seemingly out of nowhere, the new vice president at Philips managed to change my attitude overnight when he decided to evaluate my work performance without visiting my territory or looking at my numbers. It seemed he had only evaluated the color of my skin when he told the product managers in a meeting that I had been doing poorly. I lawyered up and went to war. When the dust cleared, the VP and his boss, who was also a few months into the job, had been fired.

I knew the minds I was dealing with in my sales region. Prejudice was alive and well in the Northeast in the eighties, even though it was swept under the rug, and everyone pretended it had been solved until a new situation shed light on the persisting problem. The racist card had been dealt. Philips chose to deal with the situation from within, but I knew how small the world I was in could be. My professional career of using talent and my ability to get results to cover the color my skin had taken a huge blow. I knew everyone I was doing business with would reevaluate their relationships with me if I moved forward with Philips. I had to leave.

Joanna was not doing so well career-wise either. She was quite creative and had developed into a first-class chef, but she often sold her meals at cost. She would drive to various locations to deliver her delicious home-cooked delicacies, and she never hesitated to park at her private fire hydrants in the city when she made her deliveries. Our family seemed to pay more in parking tickets than taxes. Around the time that my relationship with Philips was on its downward trajectory, Joanna was becoming bored and tired of people taking advantage of her business generosity. I tried to help her, but interfering with my wife's dreams was a game of Russian roulette.

We were sitting at the table, indirectly complaining about each other's professional lives one night, when everything shifted. We had always played with the thought of escaping the norm. Like many people, we dreamed of staying on one of the islands we had visited, maybe buying a restaurant.

Our daughter was getting tired of the same conversation over and over again. She was also wise enough to anticipate our extremely spontaneous decisions; sensing a huge change in the air, she wanted to make sure she had a part in steering it into a direction she wouldn't absolutely hate. Out of the blue, our daughter blurted out, "Well, if you really want to do something crazy, move to Costa Rica!" She'd just given us permission to move to paradise.

Chapter 9

A TWO-WEEK VISIT TO COSTA RICA CONVINCED US THAT IT WAS THE perfect place to escape and heal our mental wounds. I walked away from a great job. We put the house on the market, sold off what we could, and put the rest of our personal items in storage. Our bags waited next to our devastated twelve-year-old neighbor until the taxi arrived to bring us to the airport.

Our sixteen-year-old daughter never thought we would actually take her seriously and pull the trigger. Maybe she thought she was being cool when she suggested the move. She knew we were a little bit, if not completely, off-the-wall. Her demeanor remained silent and calm, but a major rash broke out on her face on moving day. She was absolutely miserable saying final goodbyes to her friends.

We were off to paradise without doing one bit of responsible investigation into how we might successfully settle in Costa Rica. Joanna wanted a bed-and-breakfast; I wanted a very small restaurant or bar. However, the first thing on our list was to enjoy living the dream by drinking Johnny Walker Black under the shade of a palm tree at the beach. We wanted to master the "Pura Vida" lifestyle of Costa Rica. We were determined to leave all the negative parts of our lives in the United States. I tried very hard to eliminate from my memory Joanna's father's last words before our move to Costa Rica: "Why do they always do everything ass-backwards?"

Chapter 10

OUR SIX-HOUR FLIGHT TO COSTA RICA LANDED AT JUAN SANTAMARÍA International Airport in the capital city of San José in the middle of the day on November 14, 1999. My family couldn't have been more ecstatic as we descended the stairs from the airplane and walked a short distance to the little patched-up shack that contained the customs checkpoint and baggage claim. The shack was very hot. We were all sweating profusely as we looked among the scattered bags for ours. Customs stamped our passports, and we gathered our ten bags of luggage, jumped into a gringo-surcharged double-priced taxi, and rode to the town of Escazu, fifteen minutes west of San José.

Costa Rica was one of the most stimulating places on earth. The atmosphere of Costa Rica was so warm and rich; I almost felt like it was hugging me. As soon as I entered Costa Rica, all I wanted to do was pull off my first world skin and jump in. Escazu was one of the more infrastructurally sophisticated towns in Costa Rica. Snuggling up to the western mountains that surround the Central Valley, the city blended into the natural landscape.

When we turned off the highway and rode into town, we couldn't hold back our surprise at seeing cattle pasturing near and around the strip malls of this fairly modern Central American town. We saw cows casually trotting in the middle of the streets, passing by the Rolex store, bank, and McDonald's.

There was a gas station positioned in the middle of the town that seemed to dominate the town and greet you like it was the mayor. As the taxi took a sharp right, we passed a "Mas Por Menos" (More for Less) supermarket, which was the largest supermarket chain in Costa Rica. Most big businesses in Costa Rica were privately held by one of the seven richest families in the country. A very important thread in the fabric of the Costa Rican (Tico) culture, as I would soon learn, was to know the names of their richest families. I remember how very important it was for me to know the chain of command in the large corporations I worked at; the Ticos found it just as important to know the very few families who had the power in their small country.

The taxi pulled up to the hotel where my family prepared to settle into our designed for-rich-gringos apartment. The Florence family, while melting into all the splendor of the beginning of our dream, didn't have a clue as to how much our lives were about to change. If we did, we would have booked the next plane back to New York.

Within a week, we'd used our catatonic common sense to rent a house that appealed to us because of its aesthetics. It was a pleasant surprise to have the hungover remains of the twenty-four-hour blowout party from the previous night lounging around the house and pool on our move-in day. Nevertheless, Joanna and I reveled in the thought that we had chosen the life of our dreams. Our daughter, who realized she'd helped to create bigger parent monsters, rolled her eyes and went directly to her room.

The following morning, Joanna and I took out our list of schools we'd investigated over the internet. We wanted to enroll our daughter ASAP. Our gringo minds were still sensitive to our child's high school education.

We met a man from the Netherlands who seduced us into spending a large part of our savings on a fully loaded Chevy Blazer. It was very naive of us to present ourselves to the locals and seasoned gringos as the new expatriates who had a lot of money to lose.

The El Chez restaurant was recommended to us by our real estate agent, and we became loyal patrons there even though the International Police Organization (Interpol) picked our realtor up for drug smuggling. El Chez was Gringo Headquarters, located in San Rafael de Escazu. Their menu focused on a good steak and an abundance of alcohol. There was a certain family that owned monopolies and kept a tight hold on what was sold in Costa Rica. Not many imports crossed the border without the family's permission. Finding a tender piece of meat other than the *lomito* (filet mignon) at El Chez was nearly impossible. A professional golfer from Argentina, Chez was the founder of the El Chez restaurant. Argentina breeds some of the finest cattle in the world. Chez could not tolerate the concept of selling tough meat to his customers. Chez started the lomito-dominated menu, and the two Englishmen who rented the restaurant from Chez brought in the extensive alcohol menu and generous portions.

Every day, after a shower and a few scotches, we collected our teenage daughter and drove down to the restaurant "El Chez." Dinnertime in the US was around six o'clock. Costa Rican families and long-term expat gringos usually ate dinner around eight o'clock, so we had our choice of patio tables when we arrived at six. We sat at the center patio table to enjoy the very comfortable seventy-five-degree November weather. Our delicious lomito was charbroiled to order, served with a baked potato and small salad. We were delighted with our meal, very impressed with the Tico chef's superior marinade.

One evening, as I ate with my family, I couldn't help but notice a familiar face at an inside table. He was stretching his neck as much as he could to get a full view of our table's attendance. It was obvious we were being sized up. The picture came together when I remembered that he was Tabo, the Tico who had been housesitting the place we were living in with his family before we signed the rental contract. It wasn't difficult to understand that my handsome family were the new items on Tabo's social menu.

While Tabo waited for his and my families to finish our meals, a large parade of mainly gringos and bilingual Ticos migrated into the restaurant and made sure the bartenders could not rest a finger. To our delight, professional partying began. It seemed like absolutely everyone in this group had a lot of money.

My family had no idea we were witnessing in action the melting pot of Interpol's wet dream. These gringos were the heart of online gambling, embezzlement, drug smuggling, and a plethora of illegal backdoor schemes. The expat Costa Rica cult efficiently spread their money, bodies, and cunning throughout the country. The Costa Rica paradise party was on.

Tabo was a bilingual mover, shaker, and player. He thrived on consistently being in survival mode. Tabo had a sensitive side to him, which attracted his very solid Canadian wife, and their two beautiful little girls adored him. Tabo was like honey to the network of virgin expat entrepreneur bees, yet he intelligently gained enough information to sting the bees who took advantage of his services.

Tabo extended an invitation for us to join his family and friends at his table. I knew what I had brought over to Tabo's table; Joanna was attractive, and our daughter was a gorgeous sixteen-year-old. Before Costa Rica semiseriously enforced pedophile laws, every female past their first period was fair game. Our daughter was never pleased with our excessive drinking. She decided to position herself across from Tabo and between Joanna and me, protecting herself from any unwanted advances and also giving herself proximity to both of her parents to make sure we behaved.

It was on the edge of impossible to not be attracted to the business and friendship allure of Tabo and his family. I noticed the extremely high level of attention Tabo gave and received with both the expats and the bilingual locals. As the wonderful night neared its close, Tabo asked my family to join him and his family for lunch the next day. He had a lot of difficulty holding back his excitement to introduce us to one of Costa Rica's hidden treasures. Joanna's and my schedule were wide-open for any adventure in our new country, especially if it involved food.

Chapter 11

THE DRIVE TO THE RESTAURANT TO WHICH TABO HAD INVITED US WAS mostly ascent. Just before and after the town of San Antonio de Escazu, we were catapulted into the reality of Tico life. Almost all the houses and businesses were built with the very limited budgets of the Ticos. It didn't matter how they were built, or what they were made of; having a home was a Tico's most important accomplishment. Tabo and his wife, Carolina, who rode with us, had left their children with a relative just in case the adventure turned into a party. Joanna and I had to focus our attention as we drove up the mountain; the colorful flora, animals, and the Ticos who could easily emulate their ancestry from hundreds of years in the past easily drew our gaze. I felt that everything I watched seemed to reach out to touch us. We observed the Ticos sporting their sun-blocking hats while they tended to their farms, fauna, and various wood projects. Their prize bulls grazed and waited to be attached to their beautifully hand-painted carts, which were proudly displayed on special holidays.

We thought we'd seen a sufficient amount of our car's hood as we took a hard left onto a street that would impress a rollercoaster. This is the only time I felt I had used my head when I purchased a much-too-expensive car in Costa Rica. The two-way street had room for only 1.5 cars. The car going uphill had to find some place to pull over if another car came downhill. It seemed that if you approached the top of the hill going fast enough, you could take off for the heavens. I pressed on the gas and thought, *This place better be good!*

Oh, it was more than good; it was magical. The car leveled off before we shot up to heaven. We made a hard right into the dirt parking lot of the restaurant, Mirador Valle Azul. We could not help but be in awe of the fifteen-hundred-meter-high, 360-degree view of the Central Valley. The restaurant consisted of an outdoor patio and a sunken indoor dining room. The patio sat a meter above the dining room and faced the Central Valley, blocking most of the inside diners' views. We found a table in the front part of the patio, ordered drinks, and proceeded to absorb the magnificent view.

A tall, bald black man, the owner, passed out menus consisting of "*hamburguesas*" (hamburgers), "*perros calientes*" (hot dogs), "*costillas*" (spareribs), and a very traditional Tico food called "*chicharones*" (deep-fried fatty pork). I was delighted to see a black Tico restaurant owner so soon in our adventure. He seemed like a very nice person as he tried to entice us to order some food with our drinks. Tabo was not going to have his special guest order anything from that restaurant's kitchen. The owner spent minimum to nothing on the kitchen's hygienic upkeep. I wasn't very happy when I glanced over to the kitchen and watched the chef continuously wipe her nose while waiting for orders. "We are just having cocktails today, thank you," I said as politely as I could fake.

As if the restaurant's breathtaking daytime view wasn't enough, when the sun set, the lights of the Central Valley gradually lit, creating a heartwarming stimulation as darkness captured their masterpiece until the envious dawn's sun would eventually spread out slowly across the land, putting each light back to sleep.

Costa Rica boasted being the first Central American country to install streetlights. I could actually see the various installation stages throughout the valley; some areas had a dim glow, and others shined brightly. By nightfall, billions of stars danced over our heads, and millions of lights danced below our feet. We were absolutely delighted by this incredible find in our new country. We sat on the restaurant patio, enjoying the view, until it got almost cold enough to snow. As soon as we arrived back at our place, we showered, got dressed, and were off to El Chez. We were starting to slide right down into our new lifestyle.

Chapter 12

THE FIRST TWO WEEKS IN COSTA RICA PASSED WITHOUT A HITCH. My family shopped at Mas por Menos for the basic necessities. One day, Joanna and I were carrying the groceries to the car and noticed what we called a "shit box" four-wheel-drive car for sale in the parking lot. We needed a second car. I was writing down the phone number when a beautiful blonde gringa approached me. "Are you interested in my car?" she asked as I tried to control my macho proclivities.

Trying to contain the smile on my face, I told her I was interested, and asked for more details about the price and the car's functionality. "I will sell it for eight thousand dollars," she told me, "It's a four-wheel-drive with only ninety thousand miles."

I had to force myself to be polite. I could have bought at least two of those shit boxes in the States for eight thousand dollars. I had no idea Costa Rica had a 60 percent tax on all motor vehicle sales. I never paid much attention to buying cars in the States; 90 percent of the cars Joanna and I had owned were either gifts from her parents or company cars.

"Well, we're just looking right now," I replied, trying to let her down gently.

"Did you guys just get here?" she asked with enthusiasm. She wasn't shy, and she didn't want to go away quietly.

"Yes! We just moved here last month, and we are looking to start a small business here," I eagerly replied. I'm sure my freshly planted arrogance preceded me.

Instantly spotting a great sales opportunity, she chimed, "Hey! My name is Karen, and I'm in real estate. I have this great restaurant for lease in the mountains. Would you like to see it?"

Joanna jumped right in and said, "Definitely! When can we go?" Joanna never hesitated to set her mind on lucrative-sounding opportunities without evaluating them first. If she wanted something, it was best to leave the premises because she would literally smoke you out.

"I'll give the owner a call and set up an appointment for tomorrow,"

Karen replied cheerily. Karen was already on the phone as she backed her car out of the parking lot.

Joanna was very excited to see the restaurant and disappointed that we couldn't go that very day. If there was one thing I'd learned about retail real estate, it was location, location, location.

Karen joined us in the late morning the following day to meet the owner for lunch. Once again, we ascended the mountain. When we took the turn onto the roller-coaster road, I realized we were going in the same direction to the restaurant where Tabo had taken us. We waited for the right or left that would steer us in another direction, yet it never happened. We made the sharp right that parked us for the second time that week at "Restaurante Mirador Valle Azul." Destiny is definitely a bitch.

Joanna was inside the restaurant before I opened my car door. I thought, *Why the hell would someone want to rent out a restaurant with such an amazing view?* This location was an attractive draw, so what was the catch? I didn't get my hopes up. Despite the great location and fairly large size, the restaurant was clearly infested. Even if Joanna wanted it, there was no way we could afford it, especially with all the fixing up it would need.

I casually got out of the car and took some time to feel the brisk mountain breeze, admiring the view of the Central Valley. The tall, bald black owner, Herman, had a big smile on his face as he greeted us in his adapted Caribbean accent. Joanna was doing her "I want this" dance as she flirtatiously looked at me to move this deal along. I tried to act like she wasn't there in order to maintain a decent poker face.

I was fresh off negotiating contracts with presidents of the largest audio and video companies in the Northeastern region of the US. I had mastered the technique of remaining calm during these processes. I slowly walked around the restaurant. I found it interesting and kind of annoying that the customers on the patio were trying to conceal very romantic gestures under ski parkas. I wondered why the part of the restaurant with the best view had to be the most uncomfortable place to sit.

When I entered the interior of the property, I realized I was negotiating with a black "Ebenezer Scrooge." The furniture was well-built but sat bare, rejected, and without form. The kitchen was, at the very least, unnerving. The extremely sloppy and underpaid old cook had a painted smirk on her face as she danced around the aged grease that decorated the entire kitchen.

A multitude of kitchen flies spiced the food before the old woman's dirty bare hands cooked it. I felt I was on a bad trip and bugging out—except the bugs were real. I felt I was beginning to understand what type of person I was dealing with, yet little did I know I had only scratched the surface.

"Why do you want to rent out such a great place?" I asked my Tico brother who should have been arrested for serving anything from that kitchen.

"I'm tired, man," he replied lazily. "It makes money, but I really want to sell it." I couldn't help but notice that he was working very hard to present a wounded-puppy look on his face.

"How much are you selling it for? Will you wait until we have the money to sell it to us?" I asked. Now I was concerned. We didn't have purchasing money at that time, yet through all the grease, I found myself agreeing with Joanna about the location's allure.

"Well, $350,000 includes everything," he replied. "The restaurant, the house next to the restaurant, the three cabañas (cabins) a hundred meters down the mountain, and my house down the hill."

"Wow!" I exclaimed, "How much do you want for a rental of just the restaurant?" I was firing off numbers in my head. I had counted the existing chairs and tables.

The patio, which was not being utilized properly, was a gold mine. He knew we were New York gringos fresh off the rack. We were accustomed to exorbitant prices and didn't have a clue what local Tico prices were. "I'm not sure," he replied slowly, hesitating for a few seconds. "I think around five thousand per month would be fair."

Yes, I thought. *It would also be fair if we became his slaves for the duration of a standard three-year contract.* I knew what he was doing; I had learned during my travels to developing countries such as Egypt and Tanzania to always take at least 40 percent off the asking price when negotiating a purchase. The location was amazing, but the restaurant was a toxic wasteland.

"I can't go there," I countered. "Your restaurant has a lot of potential, yet my problem is that we would have to put a lot of money into bringing the property up to our standards. First of all, we would have to enclose the patio; it has the best view of the Central Valley, but people are freezing out there. The entire restaurant would need to be painted, and, not to be rude, but your kitchen is a nightmare. I can't run a restaurant that is not up to my mother's white-glove standard." I left him with one of the things my mother always used to tell me: "The kitchen should be clean enough to feed your own family." I pointed out that the amount of money I would have to put into the restaurant to bring it up to standard would increase the value of his property.

The owner was not expecting to be dealing with an executive who was highly experienced with negotiating contracts. To his surprise, I was not one of those "ignorant black gringos." Many people of African lineage from outside of the United States are given a negative image of their African-lineage counterparts who were born in the United States. The truth about Costa Rica is that they, like the United States and most of the world, have prejudice knitted deep into their culture. For various reasons, many people of color migrated from the Caribbean islands to the Atlantic coast of Costa Rica during the nineteenth century. Even though many people of African lineage, whom the Ticos called "Negros" (Blacks) or "Morenos" (mixed-race "mulattos") were born on Costa Rican soil, these Ticos of color were contained on the Atlantic coast and not recognized as citizens until the late sixties. To the restaurant owner's credit, his fluency in English allowed him to deal with many uneducated white Northern Americans who came to Costa Rica and blindly walked into cultural black holes that sent them home with half, if not none of their "Costa Rica dream money." A popular joke in Costa Rica is: "If you want to be a millionaire in Costa Rica, bring two million."

With a renewed respect for this freak black man from North America, the owner decided to put the ball in my court. His smirk not budging, he leaned back and said, "Well, how much are you willing to pay?"

I didn't hesitate for a second. I knew it was my move. "$2,500 but I want a lease with an option to buy at $350,000 with the entire $2,500 going toward the purchase price," I replied firmly. He looked me in the eye. I didn't flinch. One of the most important, if not *the* most important rule of sales I was taught at "IBM Sales Boot Camp" was to remain silent after proposing a deal until the person on the other end answers. If I had flinched or opened my mouth, I would have given the edge back to the owner. The Realtor, who had been a silent observer of this whole transaction, was enjoying the process. She was seasoned enough to know that there was going to be some kind of deal.

Joanna tried to not to jump out of her skin.

"OK," he said, feigning resignation, although I knew $2,500 a month had to be a lot more than he was making from the restaurant in the condition it was in. We shook hands, locking each other's hand with a strong grip.

After only four weeks of being in Costa Rica, Joanna and I were about to open our own restaurant in one of the most beautiful places on earth.

Chapter 13

I started taking Spanish classes for one hour a day. It was like throwing greased patties at the mucus on my forty-year-old brain. We spoke English at home and at El Chez. I was proficient enough in running a business to put together the basic operations for our new restaurant, but without being conversational in Spanish, there was no way I could conduct the interviews to fill positions. We had kept all of the existing staff but wanted to add a couple of waiters and some more advanced chefs. I needed someone who was bilingual. I had observed Tabo on various occasions, and I was very impressed with him and his ability to establish rapport with various groups of people.

A few weeks after we leased the restaurant, some newlyweds who frequented El Chez hosted a Thanksgiving party at their home. A lot of the El Chez gringos and bilingual Ticos were in attendance. Tabo and I separated ourselves from the rest of the party to discuss the possibility of him joining my restaurant enterprise as a head manager. He was extremely personal and great with the ladies. Tabo had integrity with everything except his sex life. That wasn't my problem. I was going to take on my first ownership of a business in a foreign country. I knew I had to have the right pieces in place. Tabo showed the qualities and enthusiasm that I was looking for.

I knew how important it was for me to make sound decisions. I saw the restaurant location as a no-brainer to success. I knew the renovations I would need to make in order to take full advantage of the property. Joanna had a natural aesthetic touch, which would bring together the finer details of the restaurant's presentation. I needed someone like Tabo since he was 100 percent bilingual, understood the restaurant service business, and knew absolutely everything about Costa Rica. The high season for tourism was just around the corner. We needed to get everything in order ASAP.

Tabo was accepting my offer, and my night was going perfectly until, in the middle of our conversation, I saw something out of the corner of my eye that made my blood boil. "What the fuck?" I heard myself exclaim. I'd known that Joanna was eccentric, and that both of us were sporting a long track record of infidelity, yet this time she cut the cake in a completely different direction. While I was speaking to Tabo, Joanna stood not six feet away, kissing a strange male Tico, not once or twice, but three times.

I, of course, immediately started to walk the four steps toward her when Tabo grabbed my arm. "Let it go. She's drunk; it doesn't mean anything," he told me. In the ghetto, Tabo would have to be killed along with the guy for interfering. For some inexplicable reason, I realized he was right. Tabo knew a lot more about the transitioning gringo in paradise than I did. We settled back into our conversation while I scoped out which Tica I could meaninglessly kiss that night.

Chapter 14

THE RESTAURANT RENOVATION WAS AT FULL SPEED. TABO AND I MADE a long-term agreement, which included his very competent wife working with us for six months. My two top priorities were to enclose the patios with top-to-bottom windows and to exorcise all the filth from the kitchen. I had the workers take out, if not burn, absolutely everything in the kitchen, including the drywall. When everything in the kitchen was out, I exterminated the entire restaurant before we replaced the walls. Most of my childhood in the Boston ghetto was filled with roaches; I hated them like they were my worst enemy. I still get visual memories of entering the bathroom in the ghetto late at night and killing swarms of cockroaches before using the toilet. It wasn't just our customers who were going to eat from that kitchen; my family and I were going to spend most of our time in the restaurant, conveniently sparing ourselves the cooking and cleaning elements of daily family meals.

Tabo and his Canadian wife, Caroline, were a great management team, yet I couldn't help but notice that Tabo's wife had to consistently pull back the reins on Tabo's emotions. Mark and Lofty, the Englishmen who operated El Chez, were not very pleased with me borrowing her since she was their cornerstone who basically kept their catastrophic losses at a minimum. Mark and Lofty had people skills with which I could not have been more impressed. They knew every single name that walked through their door. I think they'd find out names before they met the people. Their problem was that during their respective shifts, they would get absolutely hammered drinking with their customers as they made everybody feel at home. The money that was literally pouring into El Chez should have made them both multimillionaires. They were the perfect example of pub owners who didn't have a clue what was going on in the background. El Chez accounts receivable could have paid their rent for at least a year. Don't get me wrong; El Chez was one of the best places on this earth in terms of food, drinks, clientele, and atmosphere.

Tabo, however, was extremely knowledgeable and had many connections that would help us complete our task. He knew exactly where to find everything from a kitchen spoon to two of the best chefs from Cerruti, the restaurant considered to be Escazu's best. You were nobody if you hadn't been seen dining at Cerruti.

All of us worked diligently. The newly renovated Mirador Valle Azul (Blue Valley Lookout) was converted into a sophisticated restaurant that catered to the entire population of Costa Rica. I had Tabo translate my requirements for the staff a day before we opened. I told them that I would be easy to work with as long as they followed my rules. Customer satisfaction was the most important. Every employee was to treat absolutely everyone who walked into the restaurant similarly. Ticos often had a tendency to discriminate against Tico customers. Tourism was the largest income-producer in Costa Rica. From menus to service, the Ticos would be more attentive to the tourists than to the locals. Some restaurants would even have a gringo menu and a Tico menu, of which the former, of course, would be more expensive. Tabo and I set up a multilingual menu with pricing that would allow everyone from the poorest to the richest of guests to enjoy a meal at Valle Azul. Tabo told me that if I got the local business, they would bring the tourists.

The doors opened at the end of December, which was the beginning of high season. Costa Rica's two tourism seasons were tied to its two climate seasons; the dry season (December to April) was also called high season, and the rainy season (May to December) was low season. High season was a restaurant or hotel's lifeblood.

Chapter 15

IT WAS AMAZING TO WATCH OUR HARD WORK AND CREATIVITY PAY OFF. The restaurant was our art; it reflected our eyes, our taste, and who we were. I knew the grand opening could catapult our business onto a trajectory either upward or downward. My staff consisted of a scene from one of those dysfunctional war hero movies: an unpredictable manager, two sensitive chefs, an ex-alcoholic senior waiter, a Nica con man waiter, a silly cokehead, and two young gigolo waiters. Before the doors opened, I had Tabo translate my number one rule: "Treat everyone equally and at the highest level of service."

The renovated Mirador Valle Azul restaurant opened its doors on December 15, 1999. People from every class of Costa Rica came. I stood at the door and greeted every customer as they entered our restaurant's romantic atmosphere. One of Rubén Blades's saxophonists danced around the guests while they were escorted to their tables. Every table had lit candles and a bouquet of flowers. The lucky customers were able to reserve a seat on our newly enclosed patio overlooking the breathtaking Central Valley. The patio was still a little chilly, so we'd added two heating towers, which made it more comfortable.

I watched absolutely everything. I inspected every incoming and outgoing plate. I was pleasantly impressed with how Tabo had orchestrated the staff into a fine machine. I had not expected the high level of professionalism that was playing out in front of me so immediately upon opening; the staff was performing like an Olympic service team.

Joanna did what she did best: socialize over cocktails with who she knew and who she was going to know. I was, however, very impressed with the little touches she'd added to ignite the restaurant's romantic aura.

After being in Costa Rica for only six weeks, my family was in business. Word of mouth is the most powerful marketing tool in Costa Rica, and word about the new gringo family who had turned the old Mirador Valle Azul restaurant into a first-class dining experience spread throughout Costa Rica in a matter of days. My family's dream had commenced, yet we didn't realize the alarm clock had been set.

Chapter 16

I KNEW I WAS FAR FROM THE GHETTO AFTER FINISHING PREP SCHOOL. IN order to carry my life through the thresholds of my corporate phase on to operating a business in Central America, I had needed to leave behind the mentality of being the insecure black bull's-eye with a target on my back and my front. What made it more interesting in Costa Rica was the fact that thirty years prior to the time I arrived there, they would have considered me someone who should stay on the Caribbean side. Thanks to my life experiences thus far—my schooling and my exposure to Joanna's family and the Torreys—I had no limits. The response and respect that we were getting from operating our restaurant reaffirmed my belief that a good business makes everyone colorblind in every corner of the world.

Success brings abundant attention. We were still in our thirties, investing everything we had into our new lives in paradise.

Chapter 17

MY FAMILY'S INITIATION INTO THE SECRET GRINGO SOCIETY OF COSTA Rica was on turbo. The restaurant was doing extremely well. At night, we would close early enough for Joanna and me to race down the hill for the last five calls at Chez. The regulars who patronized Chez were very consistent. You could predict who was going to show up at Chez within a period of one to two days. The attendees included gringos who could not fly into or above the States without being arrested, a couple of foreign couples who pretended their relationships were impenetrable, and native bilingual Ticos who either worked inside the illegal bookie operations or wanted in on them, allured by the abundance of illegal money and pretty young women who wanted, in one way or another, to help the bookies spend it, convincing them to keep the booze running from twelve in the afternoon until closing.

No matter how much partying went on, I stayed focused on our business. I had to! I was still learning the language. We were paying the bills, but our numbers were still in the red overall.

After Carolina's six-month contractual period passed, she returned to El Chez full-time. I thought I'd learned enough Spanish to run my own business, so I prematurely paid Tabo to leave, which turned out to be a big mistake. Without Tabo, the staff felt they could do anything they wanted, including stuffing the trunk of the bartender's car with product. I'd been a little skeptical of why the bartender always parked trunk-first toward the kitchen in the back alley. We had to keep him because there was a shortage of good bartenders who would have been willing to walk up the steepest part of the mountain every day to get to work. We'd given the ex-owner's cook some gloves and tried to keep her around, until we found out she'd been skimming full-length filet mignon almost every night, so we let her go. I hired a young Nicaraguan woman to handle the cash register to help fill Tabo and Carolina's shoes. The gringo network consistently mentioned that the Nicas worked harder and were a little bit more honest than the Ticos, so I took their word to heart. What they didn't tell me was that if you put a pretty, young, and flirtatious Nica woman with a perfect hourglass-shaped body in front of your desk, it will be very difficult to concentrate. I would try to count the money: "One, two, three, twenty-seven, eighty-three, four, fifty-five." I didn't mind counting three times.

Pete, our security guard, had a very bad limp, and every word that came out of his mouth was mountain-slang Spanish, sort of the equivalent of Mississippi English. We treated and respected Pete as well as any of our other full-time employees. To show his appreciation, Pete one day informed one of my waiters that Herman was entering my restaurant and taking product at will. I'd never thought this man would go low enough to take from a person who was paying a healthy rent. My eyes began to see where I was and the types of situations I was dealing with. I was far away from home.

Upon hearing this, I immediately drove down the mountain and returned with a locksmith. It wasn't just because of Herman; it was also about how my bartender parked with the trunk of his car toward the kitchen's back door and how my first cook thought I couldn't read his consistent attitude. I realized I didn't have control over what went in and out of the cash register and freezer. I had thought I could trust all of my employees who'd been smiling in my face and acting like my best friend. I, the former Northeast Regional Manager for Philips Electronics, had no control of my family's business. I began to watch how some of my employees snaked around the restaurant. I started counting all of the waiters' slips as well as my own purchases and comps. I found myself spending my days in the restaurant from the time I woke up until the time I went to sleep.

Joanna was no help whatsoever. She wanted nothing to do with the business side of any business; she was a premier socialite. Joanna would point her nose to the air, or whoever she was interested in talking to, while she sipped her cocktail. I couldn't blame her; she'd inherited it. The truth of my situation was rushing into my mind *and* my spirit, which I was trying to develop into something that loved and cared for not just the people of Costa Rica, but the world. I could only laugh at myself when I looked at my staff and realized that they really seemed to think that American sidewalks were paved with gold.

I changed the locks without saying one word to Herman. It was amazing what would happen to me when I got very angry; my Spanish would improve quite instantly. The next time the first chef gave me an attitude, I ripped into him until his eyes popped out. The situation with that chef was my first introduction to a part of the Tico culture that a lot of outsiders discover the hard way: the first time you yell at a Tico will be the last time. He quit! I didn't mind; the second chef, who was his little brother, had actually become the better and faster cook. I felt like a weight had been lifted off my shoulders. My actions scared the shit out of my other employees and empowered my otherwise helpless ego.

Chapter 18

MY FAMILY AND I MOVED INTO HERMAN'S SMALL AND COMPLETELY infested house next to the restaurant. I could keep a closer eye on the business that way, especially since Pete only spoke of and did not act on intruders. The house was way up on the mountain. The closest house to us was inhabited by a man who was eventually picked up by the International Police for embezzling from senior citizens in the States. We started having after-hour parties at the restaurant with the closest of the new friends we were rapidly making. I had a projector on a large screen, and we would have concert night, playing the likes of Bon Jovi and Santana. Joanna and I were having the time of our lives, not yet knowing that the stitches of our eighteen-year marriage were unraveling—at least I didn't!

Maybe I started the infidelity signal in my marriage by going to the bathroom with someone on my "if I was divorced" list and her girlfriend. All I remember were their faces. If something happened, I'm sure it was a disappointment. I guess someone whispered in Joanna's ear, and it must have led to my big brother, who was visiting, finding his sister-in-law entertaining Roger, one of our waiters, behind the restaurant. Come to think of it, I had wondered how that waiter knew Joanna's favorite US female singer when he had given her the CD at the "Secret Santa" party.

We had brought our dysfunctional eighteen-year marriage to one of the most seductive atmospheres on earth. Joanna's father's words when he heard we were moving to Costa Rica started to ring again in my ears: "Why do they do everything ass-backwards?"

Chapter 19

THE WORD WAS ALL OVER THAT MIRADOR VALLEY AZUL WAS CONSIDERED one of the best restaurants in Costa Rica. We shot to the top of the US embassy's suggested restaurants list. The embassy humbled me when they made reservations for the diplomats and a group of eighteen generals and admirals one night. After that, we seemed to have at least one guest from the embassy almost every night. Some of the richest Tico families, private school teachers, and owners of the local franchises and hotels would continuously join us for dinner. I was great with faces, but I was lousy with names. I started a black book listing names with features of VIP clients. I kept the book easily accessible.

The employee revolving door was still spinning. The old-school guys knew exactly when to duck when the pendulum swung too close. Even though he would often come to work with XXX stories or a venereal disease, Roger had a force field built around him. Ida, my seductive cashier, wanted more control of my body than I wanted to give her; she already had too much control of the cash register. I fired Ida and hired my waiter Alberto's daughter Andrea, whom I remembered singing in the church choir on national television.

I guess Andrea was yet another person who thought I was just a stupid gringo. Feeling the restaurant was secure, my family and I went away for a week around the end of the second year of the lease. When we returned to Costa Rica, my very focused accounting routine turned up a final tally that was short by hundreds of dollars. I felt very badly for her honest and hardworking father, but I knew I had to let her go.

Costa Rica law states that if you call a person a thief, they can sue you. Andrea was not only one of the biggest thieves in my history; her father was one of my best and most consistent waiters. Their family had lived on the mountain for hundreds of years, and his brother was my Sunday guitar player. I needed to come up with a plan to explain to his family, at their home, why I was firing their church-choir daughter from the restaurant. While I was thinking out my strategy, I found out that she had been seduced by my quiet, smooth, and most handsome waiter, Edwardo. Andrea was using our money to rain on Edwardo gifts of jewelry and clothes.

Andrea's father and I set a meeting for a Tuesday since the restaurant was closed on Tuesdays. I was sure he already knew the problem, but it was still my responsibility to make sure I did not call his daughter a thief. I knew his daughter was well-educated on how to screw a gringo. On her first day at work, Andrea had arrived with what had seemed to be a history book. I was impressed that she'd brought her homework with her to study during the slow times. At a moment when she wasn't there, I walked over to look at what she was studying. The front cover read: "Leys De Seguro Social" (Social Security Laws). This book was bigger than a complete album of the *Kama Sutra* and probably better at screwing an employer. China would have been proud of all the red flags that were dancing around in my mind.

I practiced in Spanish what I was going to say to Alberto up until the moment I knocked on his door. I had learned a lot about the Tico culture in the short period of time I'd spent in Costa Rica; I'd had to. I really liked Alberto; we had a mutual good relationship. This meeting was very personal for us both. After the cordials, I began to explain why I had to fire his daughter: "Your *hija* (daughter) is a good person. I care about her, and I have a lot of respect for you and your family. The reason why she can no longer work in the restaurant is because the *caja* (cash register) and receipts did not match. The caja is your daughter's responsibility." I put Alberto's mind at ease with my last sentence: "I don't think your daughter has enough experience in the restaurant business to be able to balance the books."

There was a small hesitation before my waiter gave me a big smile. He knew the business; many things could go wrong. Making the focus of the issue the fact that his hija had been responsible for all the books gave us both a comfortable out.

Chapter 20

BY THE END OF THE YEAR, I WAS RUNNING ALL THE TANGIBLE ASPECTS of the restaurant. One magical night just before the dinner crowd came in, a tall and handsome graying-blond-haired, clear blue-eyed man came strutting up to the bar. The man walked like a Viking who had just raped and pillaged a small village; he sported a big shit-eating grin to complement his confidence and good looks. "Are you the owner?" he asked with a heavy Scandinavian accent while continuing to throw his smile across the restaurant.

"Yes, I am. My name is Tony. And yours?" I responded.

"Nicholas! Nice to meet you, Tony," he exclaimed. It was quite obvious that we were sizing each other up.

"Where are you from, Nicholas?" I asked. I was pretty sure Nicholas was from Sweden, one of the places Joanna and I had visited a few years previously on a vacation before cruising to the Greek islands. However, I remembered an experience I'd had with my Australian tennis partner who'd been very insulted when I'd asked him if he was from England. "Never assume" was the lesson I'd since carried with me. Costa Rica is an international melting pot of cultures, expatriates, businesspeople, and criminals; if you want to know where a person is from, ask them and take their answers at face value. In other words, don't push it.

Nicholas was very proud to reply, "Sweden," in answer to my question. When I asked him how I could help him, he responded, "Well, my wife and I just moved into a house two hundred meters down from here. We have our clothes, but the furniture is late. I was wondering if we could borrow some chairs, plates, and utensils for a couple of days?"

I thought, *Swedish plus neighbor equals long-term customer*. Without hesitation, I obliged him. I had one of my waiters take care of a very gracious Nicholas.

As I watched Nicholas walk out the restaurant door, I felt we had made a special connection. The reality was that I didn't have a miniscule clue as to who I'd just loaned a couple of plates to.

Chapter 21

THE BENEFITS OF PERSONALLY STANDING BEHIND THE BAR AND THE cash register, besides the full retention of my profits, included hearing the stories of gringo lives in Costa Rica. They would share about the different wonders of Costa Rica. The hard-core trailblazers would brag about finding fascinating places that were not known to most other gringos. I was thrilled to be their audience as they so passionately described every detail of places that would become my next destinations.

While running the restaurant, I continued to observe and learn about the dynamics of the population of Costa Rica. There were two sides of the coin.

One side of the Costa Rica population is highly educated and as sophisticated as the rest of the middle- to upper-class worlds, if not more. One of my favorite tables was the Costa Rican presidential candidate Rolando Araya and his family. They were very open and friendly with us. Someone in his family would grace our restaurant at least four days a week. Rolando had been quite surprised and pleased when Joanna and I had joined him and Deepak Chopra for a private lunch during Deepak's Costa Rica lecture. I guess Joanna's mother had mentioned to her friend Deepak that we were living in Costa Rica, so we got a call.

The other side of Costa Rica is a combination of people from very poor backgrounds. A good salary to that side was one hundred dollars a week, and the average salary was about three hundred dollars a month. There was a lot of unemployment among Costa Ricans because of the influx of Colombian, Dominican, and Nicaraguan laborers. Many of the young pretty women and a lot of the young men would fall, or be pushed by their parents, into prostitution, which was legal in Costa Rica, although pimping was illegal.

Foreign senior and middle-aged men in their crisis phases would come in droves to Costa Rica to surf, fish, and be entertained by these pretty young women. These men would often buy secret condos in groups, sharing the costs of their man caves. There were plenty of young gigolos who would entertain these groups as well as women of various ages jumping in the ring.

The small problem with this was the abundance of sexually transmitted diseases. The big problems began when these non-Spanish-speaking seniors became delusional about how the particulars of these arrangements functioned. They often thought these young beautiful people just fell in love with them. They would start to spend their hard-earned savings and social security checks on the pretty young women and their families. Before the seniors knew it, they were out of money, thrown out of their homes, and alone. I once had a senior walk into my restaurant with both his hands up saying, "She took everything—absolutely everything—out of my house! She even took the telephone cable!" He and his love interest had had many romantic dinners in my restaurant. I guess her Tico boyfriend/pimp had decided he'd had enough.

In these events, these foreign men had no recourse. One of the biggest problems in Costa Rica was domestic abuse. According to Costa Rica's laws, whatever the woman said was true. The man had to prove himself innocent in order to get out of jail and back into his home. The gringo abuser, guilty or innocent, would not want to be near the woman until everything was straightened out by the court.

If they could, the men who found themselves in these situations would be best advised to take the loss. Some of these guys paid attorneys to fight their case for the long term. Some would have to give their Costa Rican lawyers power of attorney to fight on their behalf while they waited in their respective home countries. In this case, they would be well-advised to make sure they had very honest attorneys. Some would change their clients' cases and sleep with their Tica ex-girlfriends.

Chapter 22

AS IT TURNED OUT, LENDING NICHOLAS THE PLATES AND SILVERWARE did pay off. He came in with his very attractive wife for dinner the following night, his proud demeanor shining brighter than the candles in the restaurant. "Thank you for lending me these," he said as he returned the flatware to me. Slightly turning toward his wife, he chimed, "This is my wife, Xenia. She's from Panama." Xenia was the first Panamanian I'd met, and she made quite a good impression on me. Xenia knew she made an impact on men, yet she played the role of the respectful wife with integrity.

"Very nice to meet you, Xenia. Welcome to Valle Azul," I said.

All of my waiters were in awe of Xenia; their eyes seemed to dilate as soon as she entered. I had one of the waiters escort the most attractive guests of the year to our best balcony seat.

Later that evening, Joanna and I went to the house to check on our daughter. Joanna decided to go to sleep. The restaurant was closing, but I returned because our special Swedish and Panamanian guests were still there.

I walked into the restaurant, and to my surprise, Xenia was sitting at the bar rather than at the table she'd been sharing with her husband.

One of my waiters turned, looked me directly in the eyes, and said, "I think your friend had a little too much to drink."

I heard some commotion coming from the patio and looked up to see my waiters trying to calm Nicholas down. They seemed to be amused and afraid at the same time. I walked calmly to the patio and witnessed Nicholas's second personality, which made Katherine seem refined and balanced. Nicholas had turned into a clown without makeup; he didn't need it.

Xenia was trying to stay as far away as she could from what may have been a fun personality when they were single. Nicholas hugged me, walked straight to his wife, and asked to fool around with her while everyone watched.

Xenia pushed him away, well aware of her circumstances, and Nicholas walked outside.

After we got the waiters focused on closing the restaurant, Xenia decided to get up and look for the wild man she had married. I found her wandering outside after we finished closing. "I can't find him," she said. I could tell she was starting to get worried. They had just moved to Costa Rica a month ago. The restaurant was 1,500 meters up the mountain from the main town of Escazu, and their house was only two hundred meters from the restaurant.

"Did you check my house?" I asked, assuming she had as it was only a hundred feet away.

"No! Your family is sleeping," she replied, "but I'll check!"

I quietly walked into our small house and climbed the stairs to my bedroom. When I opened the door, I couldn't believe what was playing out in front of me. I had only known this man for two days. Nicholas's second personality was massaging Joanna's Katherine—on my bed. To make it even more criminal, he had put his cigarette out in my new Nike Air Force sneakers. That was the day that I knew my ghetto tank was empty. If there was any time in a ghetto man's life that a situation called for an ass-kicking, it was that exact moment. However, I refrained.

There was another side of the understanding and accepting "Pura Vida" (Pure Life) culture in Costa Rica. One had to learn to accept things that would be unacceptable to most people from a Westernized culture; otherwise, you had to stop caring. All bets had to be taken off the table; otherwise, your head would simply explode off your shoulders. Joanna and I had been married for eighteen years at that point, and fidelity had long ceased to be part of the equation. I stubbornly tried to remind myself that she was my wife and the mother of my child; we were a family.

We continued to have a dysfunctional relationship with Nicholas and Xenia over the following few years. Over the course of our time as neighbors, his actions included peeing in the wine holder at our restaurant and almost killing himself racing a motorcycle down the dangerously steep hill that led up to the restaurant, yet nothing compared to the time he climbed up the outside of our house at four o'clock in the morning, shouting, "Let's go to the cross!"

The cross was a four-hour hike further up the mountain. I was still getting over the fact that this man had just climbed up to my balcony and entered my bedroom when I asked, knowing the answer, "Are you crazy?"

Before I could completely open my eyes, I heard: "OK!" This came out of the mouth of a woman whom I could never get to budge before ten o'clock AM. Joanna actually got out of our bed and left with Nicholas.

Chapter 23

"ROGER WANTS TO BE YOUR FRIEND; HE CALLED TO INVITE YOU TO PLAY pool," Joanna said, smiling at me. I was well aware of what was going on between Joanna and Roger, my waiter, but I liked to play pool. I had started making out with our maid anyway, to make it even.

Chez had lost their lease and closed at the beginning of our third year of running our restaurant. A very creative ex-con and his very conniving Italian girlfriend had seized the opportunity to provide a new refuge for Chez's regular crowd and opened a two-level bar near where Chez had been. The place had a large screen with a projector on the first floor, pool tables on the second, and cocaine for sale behind the bar.

Roger was already playing pool at the new bar when I arrived. He was all smiles when Joanna and I showed up. "I got winners," I said. Roger watched me like a hawk as I claimed next in line for a game by putting a quarter on the coin-operated pool table.

"¡Pura vida, jefe!" (Pure life, boss) Roger shouted. Roger would always call me "jefe" with extra care and respect as he became increasingly close with my wife, who was totally infatuated with him. When he'd given my wife her favorite plant, a Bonsai tree, and a CD of Mark Anthony for her birthday, I pretty much had to accept the fact that they weren't just kissing.

As I waited for Roger to finish his game, women were marching past me to the nearby bathroom, where cocaine constantly and abundantly flowed into nostrils. Joanna was paying no attention to me at all, so I was free to observe the delightful presentation. I recognized one woman who had come to my restaurant with a very rich gringo. Roger had informed me at the restaurant that she was the gringo's sex therapist. Before I could politely turn away from her, the woman locked eyes with me and did a full-body shimmy that Shakira would have been extremely proud of. I didn't move an inch. It seemed that her shimmies went through her body, under the floor, up through my feet, up my body, and into my brain. In my mind, I saw an image of me as the best salsa dancer on earth.

The woman went into the bathroom. I turned to look at my loving wife, who was only turning toward me when she thought I was paying attention to her flirting with Roger. I looked lovingly into her eyes and thought, *It's on.* My now nineteen-year marriage was downgraded to a "don't ask, don't tell" agreement.

The most peaceful moments in our new lives were when we were sitting on the patio of the new mountain home that we muscled from Nicholas and Xenia. The house was cradled by the mountains of the Central Valley. Every moment that we were not socializing, we spent watching the clouds hug the family of emerald green mountains, while the cows and bulls feasted on the luscious grass. The beautiful mountain view was serenaded with a choir of sounds from a fraction of the eight hundred species of birds that showered every region of Costa Rica. I started smoking Cuban cigars on that patio, drenching them with a fine brandy at the end of the night. I tried to enjoy the sensation of my marriage's storms in the silence and absolute darkness of the unpredictable Costa Rica nights.

Chapter 24

ANTONIA FLEW THE NEST TO ATTEND THE UNIVERSITY OF MIAMI during our third and final year of the restaurant lease. The restaurant was on cruise control businesswise. We were making money and keeping a steady flow of guests. Cruise control was kind of illegal for gringos who owned businesses in Costa Rica. That's when Herman came alive.

"Jefe!" Roger kept his head down while carefully turning it toward me to make sure he had my attention, and then he quickly looked back down as he washed the glasses we had in the bar sink next to the POS register.

"¿Qué paso, Roger?" (What happened, Roger?) I asked, trying to be as professional as possible with the man who was holding a knife in my back.

"El hijo de puta Herman hizo un acuerdo para tomar Valle Azul y robar todo sus cosas" (The son of a bitch Herman made a deal to take Valle Azul and steal all of your equipment).

I had never met one person who liked Herman. I tried to be as cordial as possible with this man who had ripped me off from day one, going into the restaurant after we closed to steal food and forcing me to change the locks. Herman and I were in the middle of negotiations to renew the lease, but neither person had said yes, no, or maybe. My family had spent an embarrassing amount of money turning his infested, grease-stained restaurant into a first-class wonder of the mountains of the Central Valley. I had to find out the hard way exactly why I hadn't found anyone who liked that man. It was my rookie gringo naïve mistake. I'd actually thought he would appreciate what we did with his property; I forgot that I was not in my country. I was a stranger with minimal rights in a third world country.

Roger continued to wash the same glass as he quickly turned his head to me then down to the sink. "No vas a creer quien hizo el acuerdo con Herman" (You are not going to believe who made the agreement with Herman). I realized that Roger actually fed off drama; his head started turning to the right and back down faster as he washed the same glass while waiting for me to ask who.

I mentally ran down a list of frequent customers who may have made a deal with Herman, from gringo bookies to Tabo, who would have been a long shot. When I got to the end of the list in my mind, I decided to satisfy Roger's thirst. "¿*Quien*?" (Who?) I asked. Roger looked up from the glass, glanced forward, and jerked his head toward Alberto before he could see this bull's-eye gesture. Alberto walked from one of the inside tables toward the bar, gave me one of his very friendly professional smiles, and then took a left-hand turn toward the balcony.

Andrea's father would have been the last person I would have suspected. How many shocks would I receive during this journey? I thought I'd grown up with some of the best connivers on this planet; I was so wrong. I was at the beginning of another wake-up call. I was still Costa Rica's bitch.

I had developed complicated marketing and incentive plans in my corporate life. It wasn't difficult to design a plan to protect the rest of our investment from this greedy Tico. The first and one of the most important parts of my strategy was to keep Joanna totally in the dark; when she drank, she tended to be too honest with everyone but me. I was able to trust most of my waiters; they did not want to close the door on a gringo who enhanced their quality of life. Joanna and I had no idea how famous we were becoming in Costa Rica, and I was about to make us even more so.

Chapter 25

THE MOUNTAINS OF COSTA RICA FELL INTO A DEEP SLEEP AT SIX O'CLOCK every evening. If the locals heard the rumbling of the trucks driving past their simple homes, they would have thought it was a dream. When they laid their heads back down on their pillows, they would comfort themselves by knowing convoys of trucks didn't traverse the mountains at *tres en la madrugada* (three o'clock in the morning).

My black GM led the caravan to Valle Azul. I had hired ten men, including some of my faithful waiters, to help me take what was mine from the premises. I'd also hired my lawyer to come with us and bring every receipt associated with my purchases that had upgraded Valle Azul.

I did not appreciate Herman's disrespect of me or our business relationship. I'd heard, and now it was confirmed, that he was a snake. It was my turn. Project "Send Valle Azul Back to the Dark Ages" began.

The "Grinch Who Stole Christmas" would have been very impressed. We took every plate, utensil, bar stool, food morsel, and half the bar. By the time Herman showed up at five o'clock, he saw something that looked quite like his old restaurant. After Herman saw what had transpired, he definitely lost his "Pura Vida" composure.

"Take my things off those trucks!" he screamed. He was actually looking me in the eye and ordering *me* to take *my* things off of the trucks.

"My lawyer is over there," I responded with enjoyable confidence. "Costa Rica law says that it is legal for me to take what I bought for the restaurant. Do you want to see the receipts?"

Herman looked around, unable to fathom that this gringo had covered all of his bases, including taking the belongings he'd wanted to screw me out of. He looked at me with pure anger. "Take my things off of those trucks!" he repeated.

"If you want to fuck with me, I'll take the fucking windows that I put in."

Herman's arrogant demands for me to give him my inventory woke up the ghetto in me. I started to pull out the windows until, out of the corner of my eye, I saw Hermon grab two of my full bottles of wine and walk toward me with the bottles lifted above his head.

I'd had enough. I pulled my gun out of my pocket and pointed it right at Herman. Some of the workers froze; the others dove under tables. I briefly looked at my lawyer, who contributed a nervous laughter. The gun was no more than six inches from Herman's head. I spoke with the confidence of a man who was tired of being fucked: "What are you going to do? Your choice!" I was not going to let this man hurt me in business or in life. I held the gun straight to his head. Maybe it was the sleep deprivation, the stress of running a business while constantly being cheated by those I'd thought I could trust, or being cheated no less in my marriage. Maybe it was the feeling of insecurity that came with the thought that Joanna's father had been right about the lack in my entrepreneurship skills. Everything that had built up my frustration over the years pushed me to make my final decision; if Herman took one more step toward me to hit me with those bottles, I was going to kill him.

The trucks drove straight to the storage units I had previously reserved.

Joanna woke up to the news that the Valle Azul era had come to an end; she heard many versions of the story, but she was never sure what really happened.

Roger became a lot more cautious about his relationship with Joanna from then on. It was now time for Joanna and me to heal our relationship and pretend to enjoy our time together in the unpredictable and uncensored "Pura Vida" atmosphere of Costa Rica. Joanna and I felt we had a handle on life in Costa Rica after three years of doing business in what her family in the States considered to be a wild jungle. We continued to walk through our journey ass-backwards while trying to retain what we had left mentally and physically.

Chapter 26

IN THE DAYS AND WEEKS FOLLOWING THE ABRUPT END OF THE VALLE Azul era, I realized I just wanted to play tennis and melt into the woodwork of Costa Rica, blending in for a change rather than standing out. I developed a great friendship with my Australian tennis partner. Raymond was a retired cultural anthropologist and professor from Australia. He had retired from a university in New York, where he'd lived for twenty years, and with my knack for history, we had quite a bit in common. Raymond lived close to Valle Azul and had shared the joy of our restaurant with all of his comrades.

I don't remember how our conversations turned into tennis games, but Raymond and I ended up hitting the ball at the Tico tennis club at least three days a week. The tennis club became the savior of my sanity. This tennis club had no snobs. The players included people from all walks of life, from Tico cab drivers to doctors. Expats and gringos were more than welcomed, especially if you tried to speak Spanish. Raymond and I spent many hours playing tennis, eating lunch, and having deep conversations about world history and religion. I was a little jealous, yet impressed, with Raymond's Spanish; he could understand and joke with the Ticos. No matter what happened in my Costa Rica life, Club Bella Horizonte was the place I would always go to get a pat on my back.

Chapter 27

PLAYA JACO (JACO BEACH) HAD A VERY ALLURING AND UNINHIBITED jungle terrain before the major developers from Europe and the US came and built a bunch of highly profitable condos. Everyone there was an interesting trailblazer searching for gold, peace, or freedom.

It was too late for Joanna and me to get our heads on straight; we were happy to maintain a thirty-degree tilt. If our relationship had anything left, it was a twenty-year commitment of toleration. Our love never left, but we dove into the passion of living in the tropics of Costa Rica. Joanna and I spent most of our beach time at the Hotel Cocal. It was in the center of Jaco, so we could walk to most of Jaco's restaurants and bars from there. We would usually spend happy hour at Cocal's bar.

The previous owner of the bar at which I'd met up with Roger for pool approached us one afternoon as we were once again enjoying happy hour at our favorite Jaco hotel bar. We knew Richard was a conniving snake from our conversations with him back at El Chez, but he was a charming one. He was a seasoned jailbird who often came up with innovative escape ideas. His group of friends consisted of his Italian girlfriend and his previous cellmates. Richard was a free man at the time, but he always had a case coming up. At least he was a lot smarter than the Italian man who'd had a great job managing the hot Crocodile Bar in Jaco—until he got caught trying to smuggle a couple of kilos of cocaine back to Italy. The Italian is either still in one of the worst jails in Central America or dead.

Richard walked confidently up to the bar, smiling like the short kid who was the head of my local gang in Boston, and shot right to the point: "Hey, guys! I have the perfect place to put a bar." Richard was the epitome of salesmanship; he put on a big smile and waited for a response.

I had already been beaten up pretty badly during my first three years in Costa Rica. I just wanted to enjoy some of that "Pura Vida" life that I'd heard about.

Howard's party-animal daughter immediately jumped at the opportunity, as always, and said, "Let's go!" I wasn't surprised, and I knew better than to even try to counter her reaction. Just like when she went to see her lovers, she was going to go with or without me.

The building was actually walking distance from the hotel; it only took two minutes before we pulled up to a unique two-story white building close to the center of Jaco. A Subway sandwich shop was the dominating feature of the first floor, showing up the four other businesses that occupied the other rental spaces. The second floor sported Roman roof-support columns, each spaced about ten feet apart. I was not on board with this new adventure as we climbed the stairs to the second floor.

The fascinating thing about Costa Rica is that it's a perfect illustration of the saying that life is one huge box of chocolates, and you can be sure that you never know what you will get.

Tornino saw us coming from where he stood at the top of the stairs to the second floor. I'm sure Richard had given him our profiles before we arrived. He looked like Santa Claus's Italian "black sheep" little brother. Tornino's small eyes twinkled like the stars, his smile larger than his face as his cigar rotated, inseparable from his mouth.

"*Bueno, bueno. ¿Cómo estás? Bienvenido,*" he greeted us as we arrived at the top of the stairs. Tornino was one of the friendliest Italians I'd ever met. He waved to us, signaling for us to come inside to view his brand-new empty masterpiece. The second floor of the new Italian temple was not separated into smaller units like the first floor; it had been designed for one business to completely fill in the floor. The Roman pillars holding up the roof left the room open to the breeze from the very nearby Jaco Beach. This open main room was separated from a back room by a six-foot bridge.

As Torino showed us around his property, I could tell there was something very real about him; I felt he was all business. He mixed his Italian with Spanish. I'd been getting pretty confident with my Spanish, but I had to dig extremely deep to understand him.

I was in a stressful situation, trying to understand Tornino's Spanish while being pressured by Joanna and Richard to negotiate a lease to go back into the service business. I desperately wanted to make a polite exit and get back to happy hour and our "ass-backwards" relationship.

"Isn't this place great?" Richard said. "The bar can be here, we can put high tables here and regular tables and chairs there, and pool tables here and in the back area."

I liked the place, but I was trying to keep my "abused gringo" blinders on since I was still mentally healing from the loss of my first business. I could almost feel Joanna vibrating behind me. I turned to her and asked, "Do you really want to do this?"

Without hesitation, and at no surprise to me, she blurted a resounding, "Yes!"

"This one could kill us," I said. I decided to be just as adventurous as Joanna was in that moment. Maybe my subconscious knew that we were already dead, but my stubborn conscious still refused to accept it.

I opened my mind to the next business prospect and began to join Richard in the creation of Onyx bar. I was very competitive. If I decided to join a game, I was determined to win. A lot of people in the area started problems because they would eventually get very bored at "just-drinking" bars. Joanna and I always preferred going to a bar that had Roger at a pool table. Thus, I was 100 percent in agreement with Richard on the pool tables. Attending Boy's Club when I was young had made me an above-average pool player, and I had my father's "ladies' man blood"—the only thing my father had left me.

It may have been a little arrogant, which I was getting very comfortable with, but I completely took over the presentation of Richard's and my new bar. Since I thought good pool players wanted and needed to be seen, I decided to put most of the pool tables in the back, but I put a couple in the main bar area, in a space off to the side yet very visible to all of the guests.

Jaco was extremely hot—even at night. The breeze was rare and not predictable. I was fine with the heat in the day, but I wanted relief at night. I thought we should create our own ocean breeze by putting fans at every pillar. Ticos have a good team and are crazy about *fútbol* (soccer). I decided to hang a TV on every pillar and put a 150-inch projector screen over the bar that would be visible from the street.

I was fascinated with driftwood furniture, which had been designed by some of the most creative furniture artists in Costa Rica. I decided that all the seats and tables in the bar area would be driftwood. Richard did not seem to mind my taking over on the interior design; he seemed to agree with my taste, and he was very proud of himself for convincing us to join him in his new vision. Richard consistently supervised the workers at the bar while all the work was being done.

Tornino was so impressed and happy with what I'd done to the space, and he took us up another level and had his crew cover the cement bar with driftwood. It was ingenious and beautiful. The only request Tornino had for us was to put the name of his favorite girlfriend on the side of the bar.

Tornino and I negotiated a three-year rental contract with an option to buy while Joanna and Richard continued to walk around our new bar.

I could not help but to be excited about running a business on the beach. I loved the fact that the bar was an open space on the second floor. We were given a generous gift from Joanna's parents, so we had sufficient funds to purchase the equipment needed to fulfill the fanatic ideas Joanna, Richard, and I came up with for the bar.

I thought the driftwood was wonderful material for all of the furniture in the bar. The great thing was that the main factory for the furniture was two miles up the street from the bar, right before you'd hit Playa Hermosa (Beautiful Beach). Playa Hermosa lived up to its name; the power of the ocean was proudly represented there, as forty-plus-foot waves consistently danced and crashed into the shores of the beach. Surfers paid their last pennies to enjoy this Central American surfer heaven. International surfing competitions and beautiful people were the standard at Playa Hermosa.

I secured a black-market satellite system for the bar that had all the local and most of the US channels. I was well-educated on the basic sport channels a bar would need in order to not be empty when American and international football was playing. Costa Rica Ticos lived, breathed, and bled fútbol. There were two extremely important times to have fútbol playing on the TVs at a bar in Costa Rica: during the World Cup and anytime Saprissa played against La Liga. There were more than just these two teams in the Costa Rican fútbol league, but Saprissa and La Liga had the largest and most intense rivalry.

Valle Azul had had very few televisions. I would have to be in the restaurant and in my waiter's faces just to get them to work when these two teams were playing. Whatever business you had in Costa Rica, the little bar around the back alley with the tiny television hanging in the upper corner would vacate your business when Saprissa played against La Liga if you did not have TVs.

At this point, Joanna and I were taking what I now call an affair-break; we were invested enough in the new bar to put all the distractions and outsiders on hold. Most of the days we spent preparing our new bar, we would end together at the same place with the same El Chez cult.

One of the waitresses who had worked at El Chez was inquiring about the new bar. When she asked what it was called, I realized we had never taken the time to name our new project.

"I have no idea," I replied. I had been in Costa Rica long enough to understand that everything had to make "Tico sense." I couldn't name the bar; I needed a Tico or Tica to name the bar. I knew that this waitress had been in the industry way before she'd turned eighteen, and she was well-respected and sincere. I told her I'd give her a hundred dollars to come up with a name.

She took a moment to ponder before responding, "How about *Onyx*?"

Another thing I was learning as a result of my time in Costa Rica is that life has a weird sense of humor. Onyx is my favorite stone. If I buy any piece of jewelry, it has to have onyx.

Thus, I was out one hundred dollars, and we ordered the big neon sign for bar "Onyx."

We really wanted to show off the best of what we could create in our new country. Richard managed Onyx; he didn't spend a cent in the process of creating the business, but he was just as passionate as I was about its creation.

We were short a liquor license. Licenses were not price-controlled and had an average asking price of $125,000. One of Jaco's top Realtors, who was paying a lot of attention to us and our money, approached us with a deal. She told us that a three-story property, which had a Peruvian restaurant connected to it, close to Onyx, was up for sale with a liquor license included for $350,000. The owner of the property had been involved with a murder and needed to get out of town immediately.

We had sold our beautiful home in Westchester County, New York, and Joanna's father had given us an early security account. I knew it was more for her and our daughter's security, but I'd donated twenty years of working in corporate jobs to our family, so guilt was not on the table for me in using the funds to close the deal.

During our meeting with the Realtor, I could not be sure if sex or gossip turned her on more; her eyes lit up as she shared with us the tragedy of what had ensued with the Peruvian restaurant owner: "Well, this sixteen-year-old very pretty girl was sleeping with David, the owner of the property for sale.

They broke up, and she started sleeping with a guy named Junior. David was jealous and went to visit Junior with a gun. Junior was able to somehow get the gun from David, tie him to a tree, and use a bat to send him to his first near-death experience. When David could make a phone call from his hospital bed, he called Olman, a man who owed him $50,000. Olman invited Junior over to his house for dinner, and when Junior entered, Olman shot him in the leg. Junior died. Olman did not mean to kill Junior, but he was arrested for murder. Olman knew he would be killed if he stayed in jail too long, so he started to talk. David has a young son whose mother has passed; he needs to sell and get the hell out of the country with his little boy ASAP. Here's where you come in: David has agreed to sell the property and his liquor license to this guy named Russel for $350,000, but Russel is having trouble coming up with the money, and on top of that, David hates him."

Joanna and I were very accustomed to dealing with assholes. Murderers were not exactly on the agenda. Yet we decided to move forward. A meeting was set up with David.

David was as normal as a "surfer dude" could be: blond, from California, and ruggedly handsome. We watched as his little boy absorbed the abundance of attention his father gave him. I relaxed, and Joanna was fascinated. *Who am I to judge?* I thought. I unlocked the subconscious part of my mind that had been hiding the fact that my father had shot a man to death in the middle of a full bar. The difference between David and my father was that Pop had executed a direct hit.

David and I got right to the point. Joanna at least respected me for my negotiation skills and stayed in the background of the conversation. My negotiation training didn't come from the universities; it came from IBM and my experiences buying souvenirs in Africa, Egypt, Morocco, and Turkey. Negotiations had also come in very handy when I'd had to position myself to fit in at my Connecticut boarding school.

I offered David $225,000 in cash, delivered within one week. We needed the liquor license at $125,000. I knew he'd bought the land and built the three-story building that housed the restaurant twenty years ago at an estimated $75,000. David was very close to being indicted for murder. The other offer he'd received was for more, but our prompt cash offer would help him avoid justice with a $225,000 new life for him and his little boy.

David considered my offer for about thirty seconds, looked at me, and said, "Are you sure you can get me the money in a week?"

I looked him directly in the eye. "Yes," I replied. "I will guarantee it. Deal?" I looked directly at him and went silent.

"OK!" he said. "You guys seem like good people, and I hate that asshole Russel. Let's do it!"

Joanna and I were ecstatic; the property, which we'd refer to as the "white building," was in a great location, and the included $125,000 liquor license was movable and could be used for Onyx. We found paying renters who would occupy the third-floor apartment and the restaurant.

Once our liquor license was squared away, we hired three bartenders, three pretty European waitresses, and three pretty Tica waitresses. A couple of thousand dollars stocked the bar, including a private Johnny Walker bottle locker for our high-end customers. The liquor company smelled blood and gave us first-class invitation cards for our grand opening. Richard hired some of his jail mate friends to do security; why not? Criminals know criminals.

Joanna and I were determined to run the first "clean" bar in Jaco. The "working girls" pretty much ruled Jaco; they were a vital part of Jaco's culture. Our compromise was to allow working girls in if, and only if, they had a date. There were many hotel guests and locals who had no time-out place to go to take a break from the constant attention of the working girls. Joanna and I also appreciated a time-out place every time we stumbled through the fog of actually trying to embrace what was left of our marriage.

I greeted absolutely everyone at the door on the night of the grand opening, just as I had done with our first venture. The saxophone player performed, swooning the mayor, hotel and restaurant owners, Realtors, and tourist guides on their way to their seats. The best sushi chef in Jaco was busy making his best presentations, and the staff hurried to quench our guests' thirst.

The staff proudly sported their new Johnny Walker Black uniforms; they were seasoned enough to realize that something very special was happening. The grand opening of Onyx was one of the proudest days of Joanna's, Richard's, and my lives.

Chapter 28

ONYX BECAME AN OVERNIGHT SENSATION. JACO WAS FULL OF BARS THAT never upgraded and squeezed pennies out of pennies; those bars went empty practically overnight. Onyx had the best DJ in town to round off our amazing staff. Our three bartenders were experts in making very high-profit-margin cocktails. My bartenders from Valle Azul used to remind me that tasty and sexually named cocktails made the ladies very flirtatious. It was true! The icing on the cake was when Prince Albert of Monaco graced us with his presence. I cordoned off part of Onyx and put my best security guards in front of Prince Albert and his entourage.

I was tired of being surrounded by criminals. Richard made a food-delivery deal with the hotel across the street to cover the food service requirements that liquor-serving establishments in Costa Rica had to fulfill. We would sell the hotel's food to our customers through our POS system, and hotel personnel would deliver it when it was ready. I knew Richard had left me out of the commission he was making from the deal with the hotel. I decided to retire Richard three months into the Onyx operation and gave him a $5,000 pension to start his next business.

I didn't want to be at the bar 24/7. Staying on location in the service industry in Costa Rica demonstrated obvious concern over protecting one's assets, but it was also tedious. I consulted with Tornino to see if he knew someone who could be a trusted manager. I eventually hired a Colombian named Fabio. Fabio was smart, handsome, and the epitome of charm. He had lived with his wife in Jaco long enough to know who was who. I appreciated his support and the respect he gave me for always trying to support small businesses. We had a great relationship, and I trusted him to watch over the bar a few days a week so I could have days off. Fabio had been managing the bar on the day Joanna and I received a surprise visit from Roger at our home.

Joanna and I were the talk of the town, and our relationship had begun to recover some of the glimmer it once had—until Roger surprisingly showed up in Jaco.

"Look who I bumped into," Joanna said as Roger came through the front door of our home with her.

"Where did you find him?" I politely asked as I shook his hand.

"On the main street in Jaco center," Joanna replied, very happy to insult my intelligence.

"Bienvenido, Roger! Como estás?" I said. My mother had tried very hard to make me a gentleman under any and all circumstances.

I had made an acquaintance with a Canadian gentleman named Ryan during one of the pool tournaments I'd held at Onyx. I had no idea what he actually did. Ryan presented himself as a jack-of-all-trades, which I, being an ex-ghetto kid, equated to being a con man. He would constantly frequent the Beetle Bar (a hooker joint), the Tico-owned fried chicken hut, and Onyx, going from one of these places to another.

Joanna and I had an affection (or affliction) for lost puppies, and they knew it. Ryan just so happened to arrive for a visit a few minutes after Joanna walked in with Roger. All of us sat out by the pool and exchanged stories of our lives in Costa Rica. I was tired and went to bed around one o'clock. I was hoping Joanna understood what I knew about her and Roger and would follow me to bed.

At two, Joanna slowly opened the bedroom door and peeked in.

"Come to bed," I said, surprising her, as she had thought I'd been asleep.

"Roger and Ryan are still here. I'm not tired," Joanna responded.

At three, Joanna slowly opened the bedroom door.

"Come to bed," I said, surprising her again.

"They're still here. I'll come to bed soon," Joanna responded.

At four, Joanna slowly opened the door. "Come to bed, Joanna," I said firmly.

Joanna closed the door and returned to where Roger and Ryan were sitting by the pool.

Roger was in the hospital by five o'clock. I tried very hard to avoid violence at all costs, but there was only so much this "Buddha" could take.

When you win, you lose. Kicking Roger's ass made him vulnerable—and thus more attractive to Joanna.

Joanna was miserable, and the combination of her feelings for Roger, the inequities of Jaco, and our broken relationship was beginning to make it very difficult for her to justify our marriage. She would take out her anger on any hooker who entered Onyx—even if they came in with three extremely well-dressed Colombian men. Thank God I now spoke Spanish. I was able to calm them down before who knows what would have happened.

Joanna started to spend a lot more time at our home near the restaurant in San Antonio de Escazu.

The next time Joanna and I were together in Jaco, the Realtor who had set up the white building and liquor license sale came to visit us with another steal.

Jaco real estate had been "full speed ahead" until the Brothers and the Cubans had disappeared. The Brothers and the Cubans were the investment opportunities of the century; 75 percent of the expats and 30 percent of the middle-class Ticos made the minimum investment of five thousand dollars into these accounts, which paid out 36 percent a year in interest. The Brothers had been in business for at least twenty-five years. They had solidified three-quarters of a billion dollars in trust throughout Costa Rica. Their customers could either pick up their interest every month or reinvest it to build up their principle.

Joanna and I had decided to invest an amount we could afford to lose in the Brothers in 2000 after the clerk at the Brothers' office had explained to us the investment opportunity and fielded extensive questioning on our part. The following month, we started receiving the 36 percent interest while maintaining our principal investment.

I had been at the Brothers every single month for the past two and a half years, and it had been wonderful. Yet just like Noriega with the United States, the Brothers must have pissed off the wrong person. One day, the Canadian Mountie Police informed the Costa Rica authorities that the Brothers were washing drug money. The next week, the Brothers disappeared and transferred $750 million to a secret place that will never be found. The Cubans' $500 million followed. The bottom dropped out from thousands of lives. Some people had invested for years without taking the monthly interest; they had their life's savings in those accounts and were shifted into poverty overnight. A lot of these expatriates had to return home and live with their children. This, by the grace of God, had been one of the only business deals with which Joanna and I had played it safe. We were in a position to take advantage of the disaster.

The Realtor told us there was a property at the corner of Main Street and the first entrance of Jaco. The owner/operators were going back to Canada as a result of their investments suddenly disappearing and would sell the building for a good price. It also had a liquor license.

We really did not need the property. People mostly walked in Jaco, and it was very difficult to get them to go out of their way to go to a bar or restaurant. However, liquor licenses were now going for $250,000; they were a better investment than real estate.

Onyx was on cruise control; all we needed to do was entertain our customers. Joanna was bored and spent minimum time in Jaco. Even though our relationship was extremely damaged, I still loved her. I thought that if we created a business that was focused on her, maybe I could keep her in Jaco while we put more Band-Aids on our relationship.

"OK, $225,000, no more and no less," I said.

The Realtor came back to us the same day with a contract.

After a month and an immense amount of restoration, "Fusion Restaurant and Bar" was born, with Joanna as the first chef. Fusion shook the town as Jaco's first live music bar.

There wasn't much high-end musical talent in Costa Rica; we had to pay dearly for the talent that we scouted. Our daughter was now married to a Miami up-and-coming rapper who told me that his friend Pitbull would like to join them to travel to Costa Rica and do a show at Fusion. My manager and I offered to pay for the plane tickets and hotels. It was a no-brainer to pay for my daughter and son-in-law. I had never heard of Pitbull, but we paid for the ticket so we could put on multiple talents that weekend.

Jaco was excited about real American rappers coming to Fusion. We had installed a great sound system in the bar, and we were ready for any live music show. My son-in-law called as we were planning the show and said, "Pitbull will not come unless you pay for his manager."

I could not believe the arrogance of this rapper named Pitbull. I'd never heard of him and was too arrogant at that point in my life to do my homework. Joanna only wanted to design eclectic meals; I still ran the administration of both our venues, my marriage was more on the rocks than ever, and sex was at a minimum to none—along with my patience. I said the words that I will regret for the rest of my life: "Nope! Forget it! Who the fuck does this Pitbull think he is?"

Chapter 29

THE NEW MANAGER I'D HIRED AT ONYX HAD A FAMILY EMERGENCY THAT sent him back to Colombia. I was opening and closing both businesses by myself. My total employee count for both places was holding at thirty-five. My only free time was when I went to the bathroom.

Brian was my talent scout for music shows at Fusion; he was an African Canadian who sported long Jamaican dreadlocks. Joanna and I had met Brian when he was running a breakfast restaurant called "Chatty Kathies" in the center of Jaco. It was our first year in Costa Rica, and we were bringing the brand-new Valley Azul staff to the beach to celebrate our success and their hard work. Joanna and I slipped away to have a private breakfast at Chatty Kathies, which had been recommended by a local. Brian was the chef, and we instantly became friends.

Brian and I became a lot closer as we collaborated to search out the best talent in Costa Rica. Once in a while, I would join Brian in hopping San José's live music clubs to scout talent for Fusion. Costa Rica was a small country with very small musical talent pickings. The best talent requested top dollar; since Jaco was three hours from San José, the music groups we propositioned there also wanted hotel rooms. We wanted the best talent, so we made a deal with a local hotel and paid the talent outrageous prices to show up and perform their best at our shows.

I asked Brian to take over the empty management positions at both Onyx and Fusion. We had become one of the largest employers in the Jaco restaurant and bar industry. We were doing something that was very rare; we were paying well and treating all our employees, from the top to the bottom, fairly.

Brian was more than happy to take what was at the time one of the most sought-after positions in Jaco Beach. The first thing I wanted to do with Brian was set up a meeting with the beautiful Argentinian owner of the *Jaco Guide* magazine and ask her to fill the new administrator positions at Onyx and Fusion. I needed someone honest to help me count the money that was pouring into Onyx. Fusion was not being a very good return on investment; as a matter of fact, it was putting a very big dent into Onyx's profits.

Nuria accepted the administrator position and didn't disappoint us for one minute. She had a tight Argentinian network who brought their business to both clubs. Nuria's handsome Tico boyfriend, Juan Carlos, was a very popular pool shark, hustler, and gigolo. I couldn't understand why Nuria, who seemed to be a refined, well-educated woman, slept with Juan Carlos. It wasn't my business; as her boss, I just needed her honesty and skill set.

After hiring Nuria and promoting Brian, I was still spending an immense amount of time at the venues, but with less pressure. My management team was spot-on, and Joanna was enjoying what she did best: cooking and drinking with her favorite guests. Certain people loved Joanna's cooking so much they showed up every day for either lunch or dinner.

During this time, I continued to fool myself that my relationship with my wife was reparable, yet that delusion began to fall apart the night we hired the Blind Pigs Band to play at Fusion. Dave-the-Dude, the lead, was known throughout Costa Rica as the morning talk-show host on the most popular gringo rock radio station. The Blind Pigs Band had some very talented musicians. Their English lead singer, Dave, was a radio DJ who fantasized about being a famous blues singer. The musicians did a great job of playing well enough to help Dave, another "Great Pretender," get away with mediocrity. The older gringos who comprised the Blind Pigs Band's roadie group would get drunk enough to smooth out Dave's rough edges and dance to his wannabe blues-rock music, at least until the drunken Dave turned into one of the devil's best friends.

Joanna and I had had some tough times, but when I walked into Fusion to close the place for the night after Dave's show, I noticed that something ominous was taking place. Joanna's aura was darker than the bar. My first thought was that someone very close to her had died. "What the hell happened?" I asked.

Joanna lifted her head slowly and looked me straight in the eye. I got myself ready for the obvious bad news. "Dave said that you say really bad things about me all over Costa Rica," she said. She seemed like she was going to either cry or bite my head off.

"What? What the fuck is wrong with that man?"

"And!" Joanna broke right into the conversation before I could say another word, "Kathleen said that you are screwing around on me."

At this point, I was going into a light shock. I had been working and trying very hard not to screw around on the very woman who was screwing around on me. I somehow still respected Joanna. Yet a few weeks ago, as Brian and I had been shopping for necessities, an accidental phone call from Joanna's phone had confirmed her affair with Roger. I'd been, up to that point, basically having an affair with our Nicaraguan housekeeper, but I did not take it to the highest level until after Joanna's call. I had not been screwing around before that call; I'd only been trying to take care of the business and our marriage. That call had pushed me over the edge, and I did not feel I was to blame.

"First of all," I responded, "I never bad-mouthed you to anybody, and second of all, David and Kathleen are drunk and full of shit. I don't know why David has always had a bad taste in his mouth with our relationship." I actually knew why; David was an "English snob" who wanted all the rich women of Costa Rica under his control, but it was not the right time to share this.

I was tired. It was three o'clock in the morning, and my patience had run out. "Joanna!" I made sure I had her attention. "You are looking for an excuse to be with Roger."

She continued to hold on to Dave's and Kathleen's credibility. Joanna immediately began training one of her assistants to take the kitchen over for her, and she went back to the house in the mountains of Escazu as soon as she could. My managers and I changed Fusion into a "bar" bar and started hosting discos and ladies' nights.

I realized I was placed second in Joanna's partner priorities after she didn't return for a couple of weeks. I was lonely and opened up to two very awkward sexual situations: one with one of my waitresses and the other with a working girl. Both of them found out that I was worthless when they saw me drink too much—even though the working girl told me that I was amazing so she could get paid. I still felt I could fix my marriage, and so did my ego. I even went as far as to fill every room in the house we were renting with flowers to apologize to Joanna for my actions. My unimpressed wife shrugged off the presentation.

Playa Hermosa (Beautiful Beach) sat one mile south of Jaco; it was one of the most beautiful beaches I'd ever seen in all my thirty-five country travels. The waves were huge and wild. Surfers come from around the world to compete in the many international competitions at Playa Hermosa.

A couple of gringo surfers built luxurious condos with swimming pools and Jacuzzis right on the beach, with patios watching the waves and sunsets. I decided that Joanna and I needed a fresh start; I rented a condo on Playa Hermosa and moved there from the other house.

Joanna came to the new condo, seeing my efforts to make her happy. I knew she still loved me. Nicholas and Xenia even decided to rent one of the condos as well, at least temporarily, to host Nicholas's mother for a visit, which made it even more desirable to my wife. Nicholas and Joanna had some kind of weird drinkers' bond that made them close.

Joanna went back to work at Fusion, but she made many overnight trips to Escazu. One night, a couple weeks after Nicholas and Xenia moved out of their condo, I could not get in contact with Joanna and decided to look for her. I was worried because the level at which she'd been drinking lately was putting her in dangerous situations.

I got to the Escazu house around seven o'clock. Nobody was there. I waited for a while and then continued to call Joanna. She finally answered the phone. "Where are you?" I asked, even though I kind of already knew.

"I'm down the hill. I'm on my way up," she replied.

I got angrier each minute I waited. "You were with Roger, weren't you?" I asked. I wasn't innocent; I was scared. I was starting to realize my family was falling apart. Joanna and I had both thought that nothing on this earth could defeat our partnership, yet it now felt like we were a sandcastle that was hit by a huge wave on the beach.

She didn't answer. I knew her well enough to know that she couldn't lie when she'd been drinking. "Fuck this! I'm going to a hotel," I shouted.

Joanna was silent on the other end of the line.

I left.

I could have torn my hotel room apart. I couldn't eat or sleep. I called the house; no one answered! I called the cell phone—no answer! I grabbed my bag and drove back to the house after an hour or two. When I entered, our daughter, who was visiting, was back from her night out with friends. It was a time that I was happy she had flown the nest to go to University of Miami. "Is your mom here?" I asked.

"Nope! I don't know where she is," she replied disappointedly. Our daughter was a very intelligent teen, and I could see in her actions that she, like her parents, knew the Pandora's box of our family was open.

Joanna arrived minutes after I did, walked directly to the back staircase, and sat down on one of the bottom steps, refusing to say a single word.

"You're totally disrespectful," I shouted wishing my eyes were lasers. "I know you are with Roger, but you don't have to throw it in my face. You're amazing."

Joanna maintained her silence as I walked to the living room and sat next to our daughter.

Everybody sat silently. Eventually Joanna calmly walked into the living room, stopped directly behind me, and casually slapped me hard across my head before proceeding up the front staircase to the master bedroom.

"What the hell did you hit Daddy for?" our daughter asked. The question comprised our broken family's last words of the day.

Chapter 30

THE RENTER MOVED OUT OF THE APARTMENT IN THE WHITE BUILDING. It only made sense for Joanna and me to move into the small but nice one-bedroom apartment in Jaco center.

I was always busy in Jaco. Joanna basically managed the kitchen at Fusion. I spent every morning going over the previous night's receipts with my managers. The administrator, Nuria, and I were becoming quite close through a mutual respect for each other's level of competency. I began to admire more than her intelligence. Brian would sometimes shake his head slowly up and down while making a sly smile as he watched Nuria and I try to hide our increasing attraction to one another.

The white building was located on Main Street and conveniently close to Onyx and Fusion. I could easily go to the apartment for a quick rest or an early night in while letting my trusted managers close the clubs. One night, Joanna and I decided to go home early and do what we did best: drink Johnny Walker Black. Every time we tried to talk about our marriage, we would run into an ugly brick wall. We would try to talk about the business instead. At this point, Joanna had lost interest in everything in Jaco, including me. She was miserable every time she stepped a foot into Jaco.

The doorbell rang, and I walked down the two flights of stairs to see who it was. When I opened the door to the dark second floor, I struck the small sink that was on the outside of the cement office bar. Water started pouring out by the gallons. I looked for a cutoff valve, which didn't exist. I quickly got on the phone, trying to reach my maintenance man as I searched the entire building inside and out for a shutoff valve. I went back to the second floor to double-check for a valve and noticed Joanna sitting behind me, watching the water and my panic.

"You fuck up everything," she jeered.

At first, I almost lost my balance from the shock of hearing those words. I turned slowly to witness the dark transition from Joanna to Katherine taking place. I looked her straight in the eyes. I had no time or strength to stop the words that expressed my true feelings at that point and time in our relationship from coming out: "Joanna, you're a piece of shit." As soon as those words came out of my mouth, she knew—and I knew—there were no more repairs; it was over.

Joanna left the next day for the house in the mountains. It was silently understood that her life was there and mine was in Jaco.

Chapter 31

I HAD NO IDEA I COULD CRY AS MUCH AS I DID. THE PROCESS OF ENDING my twenty-two-year marriage was more damaging than I could have ever imagined. The funny thing was that I thought I was still functioning as a normal human being even though I was crying like a baby everywhere.

Whenever I felt it coming, I would dash for the nearest private place until I straightened myself up. Once in a while, Brian or Nuria would catch me crying because I spent a lot of time with them. They thought I was being sensitive and found it endearing. I personally had no idea who this metamorphosed Tony was going to become. I felt numb, broken, and alone.

Older men warned me about "the rebound." I tried to put my head into work, but I couldn't completely focus. I thought maybe some extra recreation would help, so I hooked up with one of my long-term waitresses. That didn't work to alleviate my sorrow no matter what she tried. I felt bad for her and sorry for myself.

In addition to my marriage going down the drain, my woes began to include problems with the Tico hotel across the street from Onyx. They were angry that I'd cut off their food delivery because they would not give me a small courtesy percentage of the profits like they had given Richard. One of the four brothers who owned the hotel was a lawyer. He spoke to his sister's husband, the all-powerful *ministro de salud* (health minister), requesting that he enforce that we enclose Onyx. Onyx customers loved the open air we presented at the bar. We were only a hundred yards from the beach, and we had fans at every corner bringing in the beach air.

The Tico lawyer said the music was too loud. We insisted that the music was not loud enough to disturb the hotel customers. The minister liked me and what we'd done with Jaco's nightlife. He came over to speak to me, and I told him what we did at night to make sure we were not disturbing the hotel customers: we would walk over to the hotel to gauge the volume of our music from there. When he didn't make a move, the hotel took it to court.

We won the case and celebrated at Onyx that night. The now-angry Tico lawyer insisted that the minister come out that night and listen to the music from the hotel. Brian and I saw the two standing outside and went over to greet them. The minister told us that the sound coming from Onyx could not reach more than thirty decibels across the street. We agreed and started to return to our celebration, and Brian turned around and gave the Tico lawyer a middle-fingered salute.

Brian had been in Costa Rica longer than I had; he knew that one could go to jail for calling a Tico a name, never mind raising the finger that basically meant "fuck you." My eyes darted from Brian's finger to the Tico lawyer, observing the pure evil. Onyx no longer had an upset neighbor; we had a full-blown enemy.

Nuria was honest and pretty and had a very popular and good-looking boyfriend. We had a great vibe, but I never thought for one second that someone like her, who was twenty years my junior, would have anything to do with this broken, aging, and balding man. I grossly underestimated what my life in Jaco had to offer.

The smiles between Nuria and me started to double; she worked during the days, but she began spending many nights sitting with her friends at a bar table facing me where I worked at the bar. Nuria's features were extremely hard to resist. Her boyfriend was kind of a friend of mine, so I kept my distance for a little while.

After a couple of weeks of flirting, Nuria showed up at Onyx alone. I knew she was opening up to me; there had been a bounty of signals. I felt like a virgin. I hadn't been very successful at this whole hook-up thing, but I didn't want to pass up a chance to be with a girl like her if she was actually ready. The "rebound" warnings were haunting me. I was still crying at least ten times a day, which was less than before.

I was in a crash course of Jaco's law of love and life. By the end of the night, Nuria was still there; she lived on the other end of Jaco, and I saw this as an opportunity to see if her feelings for me were real.

"Would you like a ride home?" I asked.

Nuria smiled, relieved I'd read her mind.

"Yes, please," she responded happily.

"Let's go!" I felt like I was new at this entire process; my nerves were in my stomach. All my other affairs had been just affairs, not relationships I took seriously with people I respected.

I decided to do what they call the "Cheshire Cat." "Would you like to go to the beach?" I asked. If there is one thing I knew, it was that if a woman went to the beach with me at two o'clock in the morning, the agreement was in pretty good shape.

"Yes," she replied with a smile.

Nuria dropped her boyfriend, and we dived into a passionate relationship, and for a moment, I thought I was the happiest man on earth. I was in a relationship with one of the finest women in Jaco. She made me feel so much better about the separation. I was still crying; it was like a sickness for which no medicine existed. I tried every day to put the rebound concept in my very deep subconscious, but it continued to rear its ugly head and prove its alpha status. Nuria was young, naïve, and falling in love; she had no idea what was happening in my head and neither did I. It was the first time I'd been single in twenty-two years. Our relationship put the pedal to the medal and went full speed ahead.

My perception of Latin American relationships is that they are very different from North American ones. North America is obsessed with numbers: *How much is that car, house, bank account, etc.?* In my view, a majority of Latin American relationships' focus is: *Can you take care of me and my family if needed?* The longer I was with Nuria, the more I would realize this was the case in our relationship.

Fusion became more of a burden than a business, so I closed it and rented the building out so I could concentrate more on Onyx. I, to Joanna's surprise, started the process of divorce. Joanna used to remind me all the time of our agreement that if we separated, we'd get back together when we got very old. Divorce had not been included in that agreement.

Chapter 32

"CLOSED BY THE AUTHORITY OF THE MINISTERIO DE SALUD," READ THE sign posted on the door of Onyx. My first reaction was to tear to pieces the yellow tape they'd put across the door. It was the first day of "Semana Santa." Semana Santa started at the same time as Easter in the States. It was the beginning of Costa Rica's high season for tourism. "Semana Santa" was like Christmas to the restaurant and bar industry in Costa Rica. The States had just initiated spring break in Costa Rica a year ago, and I owned that market. Onyx's sales had gone from $50,000 to $70,000 per month during spring break the previous year.

I started calling everyone who might have known something about what was going on—only to find out that the hotel owners' lawyer had the health minister close Onyx because of noise without having one inch of proof. I should have known this would happen after the meeting I'd had with my lawyer the previous week when he'd told me that the minister wanted $1,500 dollars to construct walls or windows to enclose Onyx. I knew he was no goddamned architect; it was a bribe that I'd declined. I lacked the one skill that made one a millionaire in business: my naïve ego would not allow me to give or take bribes.

The Tico hotel requested a meeting at city hall with my lawyer and me. At the meeting, my lawyer, the *alcalde* (mayor), the minister, and all the owners of the Tico hotel sat with me at a round table. The Tico lawyer got straight to the point: "Fire Brian, and we can talk about Onyx opening."

I was insulted and very dedicated to Brian. With Brian and Nuria, I had thought I'd been protected from the mafia of Jaco, yet little did I know what and who I was dealing with. I had cut off the hotel's food supply to Onyx because they would not give me one cent of commission. I had also made an enemy out of Nuria's ex-boyfriend, with whom I'd previously been friends.

Envy raves through the world, yet it seems to condense and expand its strength in smaller countries. I pretty much owned the bar business in Jaco; every bartender and waitress wanted to work for me because we were popular and because I paid my staff fairly and treated them respectfully. I had blindly thought that putting their families out of business was "just business." This very arrogant black gringo had no idea that he didn't understand what he'd gotten himself into.

In the weeks following the closing of Onyx and the beginning of my battle to reopen it, Roger moved into the mountain home with Joanna. Nuria moved into the white building with me. Nuria was the owner of *Jaco Guide Magazine*, one of the most popular guide magazines in the town.

After we had lived together for a little more than a month, Nuria wanted to grow her business. I gave her the second floor of the white building to house her magazine and new graphic design business. The problem with my relationship with Nuria was that each of us wanted to control the other. Nuria was very different from the typical Latina who came from a poor background. She came from a solid upper-middle class background, and she was educated, refined, and owned her own business. I'm not sure if it was Argentinian culture, but she and her mother needed to be the boss. I was the boss, but I got a little off-balance when dealing with women of Nuria's caliber, which represented a very small percentage of the women who enjoyed Jaco Beach.

Less than three months into our relationship, Nuria and I started having major arguments and time-outs. I had no idea how screwed up I was. I started tripping over my entire body and mind. During our rocky relationship, I was also frantically trying to put a children's Band-Aid on my failed marriage's shotgun wound.

I was unemployed at that point; my only income was from renting a restaurant space that had been included in the white building purchase to one of the best chefs in town. I wanted to keep the incredible Onyx staff we had put together, so I continued to pay them their salaries while my lawyers tried to solve the problem.

Three months had passed since the Ministerio de Salud closed Onyx. The high season was melting into the low season. I watched as my competition installed pool tables and large-screen projectors. I had to retire my staff in order to save the minimal cash I had left in the bank. My lawyers ran out of answers. Nuria and I had a very hard time maintaining a relationship until she returned to me after the third breakup without birth control. No matter how angry we were, we never resisted a passionate makeup. My only child was about to have a sibling.

My savings account hit bottom. I was living off the rent I collected from the restaurant I was renting out. Kent, the chef who ran the restaurant, was often very temperamental, which caused his customer base to shrink quite rapidly. Many times, he was not able to pay the full rent, so I would eat many delicious dinners from his restaurant for free.

Six months passed after the closure, and it was now deep into the low season. I was down to the minimum amount of money that would support a skeleton reopening of Onyx. I had appealed to everyone with any level of power in Costa Rica. I was amazed at how much power one single arm of the health department had in Costa Rica.

I decided to take a walk on the beach and ponder my situation. It was time to throw in the towel and walk away from Onyx. I was very angry at the combination of Ticos who had destroyed my business. I knew that my enemies now included the multigenerational Ticos who owned the hotel and Nuria's ex-boyfriend, Juan Carlos. In only one year, my business had metamorphosed from a butterfly to a caterpillar.

I returned from the beach that afternoon to find a message sitting on my fax machine: *Permiso para abrir su negocio* (Permission to open your business). I immediately called every Onyx employee to see who was available. I'd lost one bartender and two waitresses. Brian and Nuria were still on board. My next order of business was to do a complete inventory and put in the necessary orders.

We opened the following weekend to a shocked and packed crowd, yet I noticed that with each passing day, the crowd would get smaller. The competition had copied my concept and had established a repeat customer base while Onyx had been closed. It wasn't very difficult to see the writing on the wall.

The minister de salud visited while we were preparing to reopen Onyx to inform me that I wasn't out of the woods yet; he told me that windows had to be installed to enclose Onyx, and he still had someone who would design the installation for $1,500. I had an architect I could hire, and my lawyer was there to translate and make sure I understood everything. However, I did not and will never believe in giving healthy people free money or bribes. I knew they were trying to control me and my business. Onyx was put up for sale the next day.

I got lucky. An old gringo who wanted to impress his young ex-hooker girlfriend offered to buy Onyx. I didn't want to lose the buyer—and I didn't own the building—but I offered to sell him Onyx for $275,000, which was the going price of the liquor license. I still owned the white building. The gringo accepted my offer, and I thought I was home free.

Tornino owned the property and had wisely put in the contract that he had to approve any purchase of my business. How my lawyer missed that annoying point, I had no idea. Tornino insisted on a $50,000 buyout fee and got it.

Chapter 33

SELLING ONYX WAS THE FIRST TIME I'D EVER BEEN PAID $225,000 IN ONE check. I decided to put a down payment of $100,000 on a future penthouse in Panama. I wanted to move there; I was tired of Costa Rica. A fellow expatriate friend, Rob, had made an amazing deal by getting three people to each buy a two-story, 2,500-square-foot penthouse at $200,000 in a building that was still in the design stage. The extra benefit from buying the penthouse was that the land in front of it, which was directly on Balboa, a neighborhood overlooking the beach, had no development plans for the near future, which would give the penthouse a ninety-degree ocean view for at least five years.

Nuria wanted to move from our one-bedroom apartment to a two-bedroom, and I also invested $40,000 in a new condominium near the center of Jaco. The owner's papers weren't complete, and we could not finalize the purchase, but we moved in and paid rent. The renter at the white building restaurant began to consistently pay rent again, and the new renter at Fusion was consistently paying as well, making our lives comfortable for the time being.

Nuria, who was now my fiancée, was thriving in her business. I had a healthy savings account from the sale of Onyx, and we decided to celebrate our newly enhanced relationship by taking a vacation to Italy a couple of months after the sale. I was very aware of the fact that Latin America had been forced to be 90 percent Roman Catholic. I knew Nuria would be absolutely thrilled to visit the Vatican. We designed a first-class trip that turned into an intense aerobic exercise class. Nuria turned out to be one of those tourists who had to see everything. Personally, I liked to see one or two things before sitting down next to good food and a bottle of wine.

We returned to our new condo in Jaco with a lot less money. Nuria went to work, and I collected rent and played lots of tennis and a little golf. The relationship was in cruise control for most of her pregnancy, but in the eighth month, Nuria moved to her mother's apartment after another of our heated arguments. I was learning that it is very difficult for two people who have the same level of hardheadedness and intense competitiveness to find a middle road.

I didn't want my first son to be born without his father. I found Nuria at her mother's apartment about three weeks after she'd moved there. I locked away my ego and sincerely apologized for my contributions to our problems, and she accepted my apology and moved back into our condo. I didn't have to be a genius to understand that this woman, who was nine months pregnant with my child, would most likely accept an apology from me.

My beautiful baby boy was born in September. Since Nuria worked, I had the pleasure of being "Mr. Mom" in the mornings. I was an early riser, and I anxiously waited for Nico to wake up each morning so I could pick him up, change his diaper, and give him a bottle before he returned to dreamland. Since my only other child at the time was twenty-one, it had been quite a long time since I'd held a baby of my own. I was very happy.

My son started walking at ten months, just like his big sister had. I tried to stabilize myself with Nuria; she was going through the hormonal low-sex-drive changes that came with being a new mother, which annoyed the hell out of me. I became much more connected to my son than his mother. As a matter of fact, I always felt uncomfortable with Nuria when she was around some of her best friends, and I felt like they were only tolerating me.

Nuria had decided for us to take a Brazilian vacation to meet her father and go sailing just a few weeks before our son had been born. Upon meeting, I could see it in his eyes like I was watching a 3D movie: Nuria's father Pedro did not approve of me. He had remained quiet about it though, and the happy family sailing trip had continued. The following day, we sailed from Rio de Janeiro to Isla Grande. Pedro must have enjoyed watching this upgraded ghetto kid suffer through the cold and rain as we sailed for thirteen hours over the rough ocean. He stayed belowdecks most of the time with Nuria, while Nuria's brother and I steered the ship. I knew he didn't approve of me, but I still thought, *Hell if I am going to show him one inch of weakness.* I sailed the boat with Jorge until the sun came up and Isla Grande came into view.

Chapter 34

IT WAS FATHER'S DAY WEEKEND, AND OUR SON WAS ALMOST A YEAR OLD. I did my usual morning routine of changing and feeding the baby, and Nuria got dressed in her swimming suit, picked up her book, walked down to the pool, and laid in a lounge chair without saying one word to me. I had tolerated it when she had returned from work and scorned me because I'd left one dirty plate in the sink—even though I paid for the rent, the nanny, and the housekeeper. Something died in me when I saw her Father's Day attitude. I tried, but I was not faithful to her. I was basically keeping my head down in our relationship. I had tried to rebound from my divorce with Joanna too soon, and as a result, I found myself in a relationship with Nuria that felt more like a business, of which I felt I should have been the chairman of the board.

I cared about Nuria, but I felt the love between us only when we had passionate sex. Men in the Florence family don't take rejection very lightly; we get very angry in a very short period of time when we feel rejected. Nuria was becoming what many gringo men said about their young Latina partners: frigid. The wild card that both parties wouldn't consider was that most of the gringos were a minimum of twenty years older than their young Latina partners, and it seemed that only after the passionate business-partner sex produced a child, the young Latina women were enlightened to their off-balance situation and realized that it was no longer just about having a good time; they now had a very serious responsibility whose future needed to be protected. In other words, the passion was replaced with planning.

I still had my apartment on the third floor of the white building, and I decided to ask Nuria for a time-out. It didn't go over very well. I was told to get the hell out. Every picture of me in our apartment was destroyed within twenty-four hours. I still see a blur when I think back to how efficiently she dumped me.

In the days and weeks following my split from Nuria, I would sit in my little apartment overlooking Jaco's main street and observe the foot traffic passing by. Surfers with their various-sized boards would pass during the day, and party animals, drug dealers, working girls, johns, and transvestites would pass during the night.

I would sit on my balcony every night and have cocktails as I watched the night's activities. The working girls would wave to me as they passed by. Everybody knew who I was and respected my businesses and the integrity with which I had run them.

There was an awning over my front door, so the transvestites made it their parking spot, from which they'd move into and out of the shadows. We kind of became distanced friends, and they would protect the white building perimeter at all costs. You didn't want to mess with Central American transvestites; that was how to risk your life.

After the break from Nuria, I thought I finally had my freedom. I was not running any businesses; I was only collecting rent. I spent a lot of quality time with my son, Nico, and I did what I wanted in my free time. When it came to sleeping around in Jaco, I tried to be very discreet at this point. Nuria had a stellar reputation, so I did everything I could not to insult her. Her big sister tried very hard to get me to return to her, but I knew I could not give Nuria the relationship she deserved.

I slowly but surely became insecure and a little paranoid. I was in Jaco alone, and my friends were the groups I had been trying to eliminate from my businesses. I had burned Nuria, telling her I wanted to stay in the white building apartment because I needed space and time to figure out why I wasn't happy. Hurt and angry, she had told me not to come back. My ex-wife, Joanna, was destroying whatever reputation I had left throughout the rest of Costa Rica. Thank the spirits I got a phone call from Alberto, my previous business associate who was now back in Panama.

Chapter 35

ALBERTO WAS THE PANAMANIAN EX-CON WHO HAD WORKED FOR ONE of my dealers in New Jersey when I was the Northeast regional manager in Philips's Professional Products division. He had been the poster boy of a chameleon; no matter where his clients were from, Alberto would try to imitate their movements and accents to close sales. My job had been to set up distribution of Philips dealers in eleven Northeast states. I had met Alberto in 1986 when the president of Alberto's dealership had requested my support of Alberto on a portable projector sales call in New York City.

I had gone out to meet Alberto at our designated meeting location at the corner of a busy street. Back then, portable projectors were forty pounds; I was wondering why we didn't meet at a parking lot so I could help him get all the presentation equipment from his car to the presentation site.

I was watching the people around me and checking out the women who were climbing up the subway stairs onto the street corner where I stood. As I was observing, I watched as this short, chubby, bald man sporting his precious Panamanian hat carried a forty-pound projector.

"What happened to your car?" I asked, assuming every sales rep had a vehicle for sales calls.

"I usually use the church's van, but it wasn't available," he answered without showing one bit of shame. My company car and thirty-thousand-dollar expense account were pleasantly humbled.

Alberto became my apprentice from that day forward. He began rising to the top of the sales ladder and eventually obtained a regional manager position at a high-tech company while I was in Costa Rica.

Yet Alberto's past had finally caught up with him. The only part of the story he would explain to me was that he had "gangbanged" in Houston, Texas, when he was young. One night he'd found himself in a car with someone who put a hole in a white woman's head. Alberto said he'd been in jail when Jesus visited him and told him he would be freed. Alberto was free until immigration did a housecleaning and sent him back to Panama without benefits.

I wanted a time-out from my Costa Rica life. After Alberto and his pregnant wife had gotten married, they started having problems, and his wife moved in with her family. Alberto knew I was shifting my sights onto Panama and asked me to share an apartment with him on the outskirts of downtown Panama. I agreed, and when I arrived to move into the larger room I had paid for, I was greeted by him and his pregnant and very unhappy wife. I took the smaller room out of respect for her. I was paying more than my share of the rent, but at least I didn't have to pay for a hotel during my Panamanian stays.

During my stay in the apartment with Alberto, I attended his birthday party, which he was sharing with a young lady named Cecy. Alberto was one of the more deviously horny men I had ever met; he never gave or shared unless he had a motive. When I showed up for the party, it was very obvious to me that he wanted to share more than the party with Cecy.

The first thing I noticed about this young lady was the way her dark cat eyes focused on her friend Rosie's every word when she spoke to her. I craved the level of attention I was observing. After Cecy finished her conversation with her friend, she asked for a room for her and her girlfriends to change. I offered mine without hesitation and proudly told her that I'd painted it myself.

As the night continued, I sat with my taxi driver friend and observed the forty-two-year-old Alberto and all of his friends who were in their early twenties. I had money and looks, but I was in no rush to jump into another relationship. The problem was I could not keep my eyes off Cecy. Everything about her seemed perfect; she had obviously taken whatever time she needed to find the clothes and beauty shops to fully complement and best present every inch of her body. Growing up, I had crushes on three girls: Tonia, who had golden brown skin; Diane, who had cat eyes and a wonderful hearty laugh; and Debra, who was smart and could control any room. Cecy, who had a twenty-five-year age difference from me, was a combination of everything I'd ever found attractive in a woman.

My opportunity to be with Cecy came later in the party. She'd had one too many drinks and felt dizzy. I was consistently observing her and had sensed she may not be feeling well. I asked her to follow me, and I led her to the nearby swimming pool and put cold drops of water on her forehead until she felt better. All I wanted to do was take care of her. Cecy was only a bit dizzy, but her friend Judy had fallen completely over the edge. I had to pick her up and carry her to Alberto's car, which would never smell the same.

Cecy knew I was very interested in her and invited me to her four-person, two-bedroom apartment on a night when her roommates weren't home. (Grouping together in one apartment was the only way four struggling young people could afford to follow their goals in Panama City). She obviously felt the same for me as I did for her, but she was not convinced of this feeling enough to give up her virginity. The following night, we went out to her favorite disco, and I was not on my best behavior. I ruined the Lionel Richie song "Hello" at karaoke, the comedian tore my gringo ass apart, and Cecy thought I offered her money for sex in my bad Spanish when I had really been trying to ask her what she wanted out of life. After that, I was cut off from any communication with her.

Chapter 36

I RETURNED TO COSTA RICA AFTER A MONTH IN PANAMA. I DECIDED I would either stay in my apartment in Jaco or go to Escazu to play tennis at the Bella Horizonte Tennis Club and entertain myself at Joanna's private eclectic-cuisine restaurant and private "Sodom and Gomorrah." I chose the latter.

Joanna had bought a large house on one of the main streets in Escazu and decided to open her own private and illegal restaurant to serve her very cheap but delicious food. The restaurant seemed to be focused on creating an opportunity for her to socialize rather than making a profit. It seemed she actually enjoyed losing money on every single meal. Her love was talking to people while they enjoyed her art; the money was at the bottom of her list of priorities.

Joanna had connected herself with every financially depleted gay expatriate in Costa Rica. Joanna emulated her mother when it came to gay men. They were attracted to her like a powerful magnet—never mind the fringe benefits of the free food, drinks, vacations, and clothing she gave them. Jonna's parents had given us an attractive savings account during the last years of our marriage, and I had signed off on Joanna retaining 90 percent of it in the divorce. Her roommates were helping her deplete that savings at a rapid pace. The Costa Rican gay mafia was her source of constant validation; they kissed her ass, and she loved it, or needed it.

In a very strange way, Joanna's house was quite entertaining, especially when the German drag queen started doing comedy shows for the audience. I think the pure essence of sacrilege was epitomized by Joanna and three of her gay boy toys when they dressed as nuns for Halloween. It will never be erased from my mind.

Chapter 37

MY DRIVER'S LICENSE HAD EXPIRED. I COULD HAVE RENEWED IT OVER the internet, but I needed another break from Costa Rica. I was jet-setting on a middle-class budget. My subconscious still thought I had that invisible net around me that seemed to always drag me out of the mud.

I flew into Boston, took care of my speeding tickets, and renewed my license. The next step was to go to New York to pick up my brother Richard and join the annual family road trip to Philadelphia and New Jersey to visit some relatives.

It was the same routine every time we went. My relatives lived check to check, more than struggling to pay the bills on welfare or minimum wage. Richard and I would spend a lot of money treating our cousins and getting drunk before going back to the hotel.

On one of the nights of this particular trip, Richard and I were going through the routine, treating our cousins in New Jersey to a wild night of drinking, when we heard some music from a nearby club and decided to drag ourselves inside. I looked up at the exotic dancers on the stage and saw one of the most sensual women I had ever seen in my entire life. Whoever that snake was in the Garden of Eden must have been somewhere in the crowd that night. The dancer presented a stellar dance performance that made me unsure of whether I was getting straighter or drunker.

The dancer knew she had my attention, and just like military-grade radar, her dark green eyes locked onto mine and didn't let go until she finished her dance. I didn't frequent these clubs often, but I knew I was now prey.

"My name is Helena, and yours?" she said with what I thought was a strong Russian accent as she approached me after her dance. Her dark hair emphasized her green eyes, and her body defied description; she was a dancer. I was two sheets to the wind, but I forced myself to sober up as I sat next to this woman who turned out to be Ukrainian.

"My name is Tony, and I think you are incredible," I answered.

Helena smiled at me for a while and then asked, "Would you like a lap dance?"

I wasn't going to refuse anything from her, but I wasn't a stranger to the dance game. Jaco was full of dancers, and one had to be very careful.

"How long have you been in the States?" I asked, knowing that any answer over six months would definitely mean I was playing Russian roulette with a woman who probably took her services to the next level to achieve her financial goals, a situation I was trying to avoid.

"Only three months; it will take a while to pay for my ticket," she answered.

Most dancers are actors and actresses; they keep their personal and professional lives separate. I became Helena's "real boyfriend." She turned out to be fun, warmhearted, and friendly. My spending budget increased to allow for plane tickets to fly Helena down to vacation with me in Panama. The second time she came down was for Carnaval.

Panama, like Brazil, shuts down everything for five days of parades and partying. It's so hot at a Panamanian carnival that they would have water trucks all around the premises. The loudest chant during the parade would be: "Agua, agua agua!" The water trucks would spray the wet crowd as they danced in delight.

Helena stood out in the wet T-shirt crowd. She was beautiful, but she also sported the hypnotic features that dominated the Central American young mind: white skin, straight hair, and colored eyes. One could only be impressed with the US and European caste-system marketing that dominated the developing minds of Central American youth.

I guess Alberto saw his opportunity to make a move that would ensure that I had no chance of ever reconnecting with Cecy. He called and invited Cecy to the Carnaval Helena and I were attending and offered her space at the house in which we were staying. Cecy was quite surprised to see me with this beautiful Ukrainian when she showed up with her girlfriend Yanisse. When I saw Cecy's hesitation, I realized that this was an Alberto setup. I was as ghetto as he was, but I was not going to follow his game. I cared about Helena, but I respected Cecy and felt she was very special. I was with Helena because Cecy had dropped me, but I consistently observed Cecy until Helena pulled me into the bedroom.

I think Cecy got a wake-up call when, about three months after that awkward night, she heard from her neighbor, who was then sleeping with Alberto, that I was a nice guy and financially secure. Cecy had the neighbor arrange a double date with me as soon as Helena got on the plane back to the States.

Chapter 38

CECY AND I BUILT A RELATIONSHIP OVER THE WEEKS AND MONTHS THAT followed. I focused my entire life on Cecy. Our relationship was solid by the time she went to the US with a contract to be a nanny and English student there. I would Skype with her every night and visit her every three weeks. By the end of her obligation, I had an affordable one-bedroom apartment in Marbella, a neighborhood in Panama City, ready for us to inhabit together. The penthouse on Balboa overlooking the ocean wasn't ready yet, and we were very worried that we wouldn't be able to sell the white building in Costa Rica in time to pay the final payment for the penthouse when it became ready.

Cecy even brought me to a psychic who suggested that I pay her three hundred dollars and bring a candle with me when I showered. I didn't believe in card-reading psychics; I'd bring the candle into the shower with me, but hell if I was going to pay that woman three hundred dollars. I only paid her fifty. Psychics do make a living, especially in third world countries. Many lives have been ruined by what I call "psychic ignorance."

I ended up renting out the white building to a very handsome and nice Romanian couple. They wanted my permission to renovate the entire building and turn it into a hostel. I was impressed with their level of forward-thinking and innovation. I offered the building for $2,500 per month, and to my pleasant surprise, they accepted my offer. Little did I know, the Romanians had done their homework; they knew what square footage would support the number of beds needed to give them a healthy profit. I should have asked for $5,000. As we discussed the three-year lease, I couldn't help but go through the images in my mind of the very high percentage of couples who were destroyed in Costa Rica; I couldn't help but think that sooner or later, they would get bitten by more than just the Dengue-infected mosquitoes.

Cecy and I rented out the Fusion restaurant building at the corner of the main street in Jaco to a renowned Cuban musician and his gringa wife. The income from the properties made us comfortable enough to move into a nice three-bedroom apartment to wait for the white building to sell and the penthouse to be finished.

It was quite wonderful living on Balboa, especially during the time of the Coastline Renewal and Renovation Project. Panama's developers decided to fill the low coastline that surrounded the city with parks and recreation facilities all around the perimeter. We would sit in our apartment or on our balcony late at night and watch hundreds of trucks bringing in beach fill while the huge tractors would push the fill into place. The coastline was constructed to its finest. Panama City was on its way to becoming one of the greatest cities on this earth, and it was a pleasure to watch the birth of Panama City's great development project.

Chapter 39

I WASN'T A PERFECT HUSBAND, BUT I HAD A HIGH LEVEL OF COMMITMENT in marriage. Even with all of our faults, I had still tried very hard to keep my first marriage together. I loved Cecy, and after a year of being together, I felt she would be an amazing partner and wife. I was ignoring the fact that she'd broken a bottle on the cement support pillar in our apartment when I would not let her grown male cousin move in with us. I pushed that instance aside as a freak thing. I had no idea how well I'd been trained by Joanna to make light of red flags.

I selected the perfect ring on Bluenile.com and made arrangements for my mother, daughter, and favorite niece to come to Panama to observe me proposing to Cecy in front of her family. I wanted everything to be perfect, so I had already asked her mother for her hand in marriage and had also given her stepfather the respect of asking for his permission.

The proposal party was held on New Year's Eve in her grandparents' backyard. I waited too long, until most of the family had left. By the time I was ready to pop the question, it was late—and I was drunk. Her grandmother, her aunt Mary, my mother, my daughter, Antonia, and my niece Tansy were still enjoying the authentic Panamanian party. I asked the DJ to put on Mark Anthony's "How Could I?" I asked Cecy to dance, and as she obliged her drunk boyfriend, I sang to her, fell to my knees, opened the small box, and presented her with the beautiful wedding ring as I asked her to be my wife. Absolutely everybody in both families cried.

I'd gotten drunk because I was afraid to propose. I knew there was a huge age difference. I was putting Cecy and myself in one of the most awkward and socially prohibited types of relationship, especially as far as people from the judgmental and hypocritical United States of America were concerned. I knew our love would be challenged at every corner.

The marriage was set for the spring of the following year at Cecy's family's church in their town of Robles. The church system is very strict in Central America; I had to convince the local bishop that I was not a complete atheist in order for him to allow the wedding to be officiated in a Catholic church. It wasn't easy working around his questions, but I eventually convinced him.

I had to attend pre-wedding classes with both men and women at the local church. The macho husbands-to-be were extremely glad when I graduated, especially since I'd mentioned that daddies should not spank their daughters because it teaches them that it's all right for other men to hit them. I think there might have been one or two canceled engagements after my statement.

Chapter 40

I'M NOT SURE WHAT HAPPENED WITH CECY AND HER PRIVATE CIRCLE that accompanied her to the church on the day of the wedding, but everyone waited three hours past the planned wedding time before Cecy showed up that day.

"Are you going to leave?" Rico, a close confidant of mine from Costa Rica, asked after two hours.

"I will wait all night for her if I have to," I said with 100 percent confidence. I knew deep inside that Cecy was rethinking her decision. This imbalanced relationship had come to its final moment of truth, and all her doubts had come together for a serious mental conference. I was also guilty of creating this crisis; I was securing a young woman before she'd had a chance to fully experience her youth. I knew I was being selfish, but I was blindly in love with her. I wanted to give her my life for accepting and taking care of my misguided heart.

Finally, the large French doors opened, and in came her bridesmaids, followed by her maid of honor. Cecy entered the church on the arm of her ninety-year-old grandfather. We'd bought the dress in New York because the same dress in Panama would have cost us the amount it took to take a trip to New York and buy the dress there. The dress was the perfect complement to Cecy's perfect body and beauty. I could only smile as tears of relief and joy trickled down my cheeks. I could not believe that I was the chosen one to be a partner, lover, and family to who I thought was one of the finest women in Panama. Cecy's grandfather gave me her hand and a look that showed he was confident that I would take care of his grandchild.

We had renovated, painted, and decorated the entire *campo* that sat in the middle of the town for the wedding reception. The bathrooms had consisted of toilets that were only holes in the floor, so we'd put toilets and mirrors in the ladies' room. Cecy had designed the perfect Carnaval-themed reception. My relatives came in from Boston, Atlanta, and California.

When I was handed the microphone to make an opening speech, I dug deep to use my best Spanish and said: "*Yo se que profundo en mi corazón que yo voy a ser con Cecy toda mi vida.*" (I know deep in my heart, that I will be with Cecy for the rest of my life). Everyone at the reception clapped with joy. Our families and friends were absolutely delighted by the Panamanian hospitality and the Panamanian Carnival-themed wedding. It was a great time.

My daughter, however, was not very pleased when the reality set in that her father was no longer available to return to her mother; it was quite obvious to the attendees and to Cecy.

I received two offers for the white building. The first offer was from the owner of one of the most popular hooker bars in Jaco; the second was from the Daystar Corporation, which found out that there was a very big possibility that a new hooker bar would be put right in front of their luxury condos. I was very motivated to sell so I could pay off the Panama penthouse. The hooker bar's offer was $100,000 more than Daystar's, if I was willing to wait two months. Daystar could close in one week. I wanted the extra money, but I'd seen many deals fall through when there was a waiting period. I sold the property to Daystar.

We made the final payment on the penthouse and bought a $40,000 Mazda SUV. Cecy and I thought we had everything under control after one year of being married—when a new baby began growing inside her womb.

Around that time, the renter at the Fusion building called and said, "The restaurant floods every time it rains. We are not going to pay the rent until you fix the problem."

I had already known about the problem. The corner property that had once housed Fusion had been a nightmare from the beginning. Joanna, my manager, and I had all thought we had solved the problem when we spent a lot of money redirecting the river that ran beneath the restaurant. It had turned out to be a temporary fix. The increasingly aggressive rainy season only made things worse. The last renter had practically needed a boat to navigate the level of flooding that took place during the rainy season.

Raul, the renter, was used to handling problems. I purchased a powerful pump to push the water out of the building as a temporary fix, but it didn't completely solve the problem. My only solution was to give the Cuban renters an out of their contract. They accepted it, but they took another six months to leave, which translated into a six-month depletion of our savings account plus lawyers' fees.

While we were doing a property check at Fusion after the Cubans left, another Realtor approached us about renting the building. This one was from a group of Italian New Yorkers who were partners in a fairly large fishing yacht organization at the Los Suenos Marriott resort. As it turned out, they were the family of my good friend Joey who'd recently passed away.

I knew Jaco, and I never wanted to return. I'd done business with many Italian descendants in New York who were some of the most honest people on this earth. Since these clients were Joey's family, I felt I had finally found the solution that would give me a solid budget and keep me away from Jaco. If I was a surfer, I would probably have felt differently, but anyone who was not a surfer and stayed in Jaco had better have been a mental decathlon Olympian who could avoid the black holes of partying, sex, and drugs. The Italian New Yorker Clients offered me $1,500 a month. It was done!

Chapter 41

THE PENTHOUSE WAS PAID FOR, AND $1,500 A MONTH COVERED ALL OF our basic bills. The problem was that I had depleted my savings by paying lawyers and traveling to Costa Rica to work with the lawyers to throw the previous renters out of Fusion. Cecy was approaching the end of her pregnancy term, and we had arranged for her delivery in one of the best private hospitals in Panama City.

Cecy and I followed the doctor's orders to the labor minute; as soon as her contractions reached the correct interval, off we went to the hospital on March 26, 2010, ready for her to deliver. Cecy was dilating when she remembered that my extremely chauvinistic brother had been born on the twenty-sixth, and she did everything she could to keep our little girl from being delivered on that day. I'm not sure, but I think her determination created a problem. On the twenty-seventh, the medical staff felt Cecy was definitely ready for a natural delivery. The doctor performed a forearm push on Cecy's stomach to push the baby out. I had not heard of or seen such a delivery in my entire life. I wanted to walk over and knock the doctor out, but I was in another country amidst another culture.

Lucy, my light, came out of her mother with her eyes wide-open.

There was a small problem after Lucy was born: I only had enough money left to pay half the bill. Nicholas and Xenia now lived in Panama and still loved me enough to attend the birth of our beautiful little girl, Lucianna. Nicholas was now a private contractor for his packaging company and was able to bring in $250,000 a year without expenses. Most of his money went toward buying a condo for his family and paying reparation costs at the international hotels he'd wrecked during his inebriated stays. Nicholas was a good and generous friend to me; he covered my shortfall without question, knowing I would do everything in my power to return the favor. Even though Nicholas was at times a frustration during my marriage with Joanna, we had created a balance of friendship through being partners in tennis and golf, and when he'd had his son, he'd chosen me as the godfather. It had developed into a very strong bond.

Before Cecy left the hospital, I traded the $40,000 Mazda in for a Hyundai Tucson and $15,000 in cash. Lucy was my third child; I knew what kind of resources we would need to take proper care of her. Cecy returned home happy to have the money needed to set up the traditional baby presentations for our newest member of the family and her visitors. We furnished the penthouse liberally.

Shortly after Lucy's birth, the family of my friend Joey started to delay in paying the rent at the Fusion building. Cecy and I were in a very temporary comfort zone after the Mazda trade-in and tried to live our lives at the level we had become accustomed to. The monthly maintenance on the penthouse was only $350, which we struggled to pay only six months after I sold the Mazda. I loved the status of living in the penthouse, but I also did not want my family to be under financial pressure. I still had the Fusion building in Jaco, which I thought was my end-all security. I thought, *As long as I still have the Fusion property, which had an $800,000 offer three years ago, I can wait a couple of years to let the value increase before I sell it, and I will never be poor again.*

I decided to take one of the "Costa Rica gringo loans" out on Fusion. I had good credit with my friend and sometimes drinking partner Mike, and he was more than happy to lend me $100,000 at 10 percent interest. I thought the loan would buy me time to sell the building and allow Cecy and me to live comfortably until then.

Chapter 42

"Tony, please go with me to get Nicholas out of prison," Xenia pleaded.

I could tell she was extremely upset. I had just picked up Nicholas from the airport and dropped him off at home. I'd been a little worried about him and his family because of the conversation we'd had in the car.

"I had a crazy trip to Brazil," he said "Xenia wants me out of the house. I have these crazy dreams of doing something to Xenia and the boys." I listened as Nicholas blurted this out, but I did not feed into his words. I knew Nicholas well enough to know not to escalate the situation.

"What the hell happened in Brazil?" I'd asked, trying to evaluate exactly how far he was falling off the edge. I knew he had meant that he wanted to do a murder-suicide, and my job was to protect Xenia and those kids at all costs.

Nicholas had given me his handsome shit-eating grin, leaned toward me, and said, "I can't tell you."

Nicholas was usually a wide-open guy with me; in Costa Rica, he'd had no problem climbing up my balcony at four o'clock in the morning to take my ex-wife hiking to the cross at the top of the mountain. After Nicholas had insinuated that he was thinking about murder and suicide and would not tell me about whatever debauchery had happened in Brazil, I had known something was very wrong.

"What happened?" I asked Xenia.

"Well, it seems your buddy was naked on the main street and decided to tackle the oncoming traffic," she replied.

"Oh my God! I thought he was home with you and the kids," I exclaimed.

"No, he was crazy so I would not let him in. He was staying at the Panama Hotel," she told me.

"OK, I'll be right there," I said.

I told Cecy what was going on and prepared to head out to deal with the situation. As I walked to the door, Cecy, with our newborn baby in her arms, said, "I don't want Nicholas in this apartment."

Nicholas didn't need a buddy or a wife; he needed an exorcist. He had flown the coop.

Xenia and I arrived at the police station to find Nicholas half-naked and three-quarters of the way into another world; he was turning into another person and seem to be accepting the change.

Xenia paid the fine, and we brought Nicholas to the nearest psychological clinic. I knew deep inside that a Panamanian clinic would not be able to help Nicholas; he needed to go home to Sweden.

Nicholas escaped after three days. When Xenia would not let him in, he came to my apartment. Cecy refused to let him come up to our apartment, but I went downstairs to address my godson's father. "Nicholas, listen to me closely: enough is enough. You are hurting everyone who loves you. You can't go home, and you can't stay with us. You have a big fucking problem."

"I know!" Nicholas admitted with his head down in shame.

I continued because I knew this was my only chance to convince him to get help and hopefully save his life. "Nicholas, you know a Panamanian clinic will not help you; they don't understand your culture. You need to go home and get help from Swedish doctors. They will understand more of what you think and take better care of you because you are Swedish."

Nicholas knew his options in Panama had completely dried up; whatever he'd done in Brazil had topped the mayhem he'd produced in Dubai, Spain, and the many other countries in which he'd wreaked havoc. His $250,000 annual payout was now null and void.

"I'll pay for your ticket to Sweden, and your wife will set up a place for you to stay. Do you agree?"

Nicholas hesitated, briefly looked at me with trust in his eyes, and agreed to our arrangement. I was very happy to be sending my friend off to Sweden the following day.

Chapter 43

I COULD NOT SPEAK BECAUSE SHE WAS CRYING SO HARD. I KNEW something was very wrong, but I couldn't have imagined what Xenia's next words would be after she collected herself.

"Nicholas is dead," she sobbed, starting to cry before collecting herself again. I was not completely shocked, but I was deeply saddened. I decided to just let her talk. "He left his friend's house and jumped in front of a train." She started crying even harder. "They are picking up all of the pieces they can find." I knew Nicholas was not going to have a normal exit, but he'd definitely exceeded my expectations.

Nicholas had passed over. He had been my tennis and golf partner and confidant. I'd named my son Nicolas after him.

Cecy's attitude in the following weeks became one of rigid survival. Whenever I chose to take the risk of being with a beautiful and younger partner, I automatically expected them to meet and exceed my needs. It was a very selfish approach, but my arrogance was well-fed by the culture I had been living in for the past ten years. I'm not a woman; I wished I could understand what and who the women in my life were, especially after they'd had a child, but I couldn't.

When Nicholas passed, I decided to not let rejection take me away from my family ever again. I was going to stay and hope that Cecy would in time remember what had started "us."

Chapter 44

THE RENTER OF THE FUSION BUILDING IN JACO STOPPED PAYING THE rent altogether. The man who was running the restaurant promised the rent was coming and continued to blame the problem on his partner in New York. Our primary income came from that rent. I knew the flooding at the restaurant was a problem, but I'd never thought that restaurant operator would fall into the same black hole as many middle-aged naïve expatriates eventually do. I had thought I was dancing around the inside of the upper circle with those renters like a professional skateboarder, yet I really had been dancing around the black hole, and it was only a matter of time before physics caught up to me.

I hated my life and who I had become in Jaco. I felt the world and all relationships only revolved around money, and it did not matter who I was so much as what I had. I wanted my life to be normal and in a box like most people did. I had a beautiful wife, life, and family. I did not want to return to Jaco—never mind bring my family—and I was willing to go to any and all lengths to avoid it.

I decided to sell the penthouse. It was unnerving to sell something so comfortable with such a magical view of the Pacific Ocean. I wanted to dodge Jaco and the United States. Panama had given me a good life; the plethora of colors in the populace there prevented me from being a bull's-eye gringo. As long as I kept my mouth shut, no one knew where I was from. Panama was a real city with a lot more lifestyle options than Costa Rica. The skyline of skyscrapers, restaurants, and theaters were complemented by the amazing engineering feat of surrounding the entire city with parks and recreation areas. My heart and soul connected with Panama; I never wanted to leave.

We moved into a rental apartment, which wasn't a bad trade. We had an even better ocean view, all the amenities, and pretty much the same floor plan as the penthouse. The recreation area for the kids was fantastic, and there were plenty of kids for Lucy—who was now two years old—to play with, whereas at the penthouse there were not. It also didn't hurt to have a quarter-million dollars from selling the penthouse to back up the American Express platinum card.

Throughout the next four years, I would watch that money disappear. I knew that when I married one of the jewels of Cecy's family, I also married the entire family. I did not have a problem chipping in when Cecy's grandmother needed a specialist in oncology or when her aunt needed an optician; I even kicked in for her sister's braces. Lucy went to a private day care and dance classes until she was four, while Cecy perfected her shopping skills. I played tennis at least five days a week and worked out with Cecy at our high-end health club. We even flew into the States, rented a SUV, and traveled through half of the country so I could proudly introduce my new family to my godmother in Vermont before we worked our way through ten other states to end our trip with a visit to my mother in Alabama. My big brother, Richard, came along for the free ride and the treats. Our life was great when we were being totally irresponsible.

The restaurant property in Jaco was becoming the pinhole leak in our life raft. I kept hoping that Joey's family would start catching up and pay the rent. Cecy began working her ass off as a news producer at a television station for six hundred dollars per month. She'd even had her life threatened by a murder witness when she had promised that his face wouldn't be shown during an interview, yet her boss had made the decision to show his face anyway. I began bringing her to work at five o'clock every morning to protect her.

Chapter 45

Our resources were depleted, and I was $100,000 in debt by the beginning of 2004. My built-in self-destructive attitude told me that if worse came to worst, I could always sell the property in Jaco for a lowball price around $500,000 and go back to the States. I was living in a fantasy world, telling myself that everything with my money was perfect. The master manipulator Tony Florence would always make it right, even though he was slowly but surely backing himself up onto the edge of a volcano.

I was the happiest I had been in many years. My kids loved me and were healthy and happy. Cecy's beauty, smile, and laugh made my heart sing with joy. I felt my heart was still safe in my wife's hands. She came from a solid old family background in Panama to which I'd paid a lot of attention before I'd asked her to marry me. There were many beautiful temptations in Panama, but I put her at the top of my priorities.

I spoiled her with whatever we could afford: Shakira, Alejandra Saenz, and Jennifer Lopez concerts; Russian Swan Lake Ballet; the finest restaurants; typical parties at her grandparent's house; and, of course, all of the best for our little girl, Lucy. All I wanted was to see Cecy's beautiful smile and laugh. In other words, even though I'd expertly handled a $2 million IBM marketing budget, my budget of the heart was completely screwing me up.

Joey's family was the third renter at Fusion who had stopped paying. The quarter-million dollars I'd cleared from the penthouse sale after paying off our debt fell to fifty thousand over the four years that had followed— thanks to the high lifestyle we'd grown so accustomed to.

The panic button was hammered, and plan B went into effect. We broke the Panama lease, put almost everything into storage, gave our electronics and very expensive bedding to Cecy's family, moved into my daughter Antonia's apartment in North Carolina, and began looking for jobs.

Antonia was happy to have her dad and his family around her and her roommate, but it was a full house in her small two-bedroom apartment. Cecy put in job applications for the local news stations and attended a church she had heard about. I paid five thousand out of the thirty- five thousand I had left to purchase a high-interest Camry so we could have some flexibility and get to any interviews that came up. I didn't know that one's credit went to hell if they stayed out of the country for too long. The platinum American Express I'd had in Panama was good for nothing in the States.

Cecy was able to at least get a freelance reporting job with the local Univision office, but the problem was that she did not have a license, a car, or the expensive equipment she would need in order to get to the various reporting locations and film her stories. I got nothing over a three-month span. I was old news and had no connections in North Carolina. I daydreamed about the times when companies like Philips came looking for me.

The money was once again running short, and I thought I could sense a little tension between Cecy and my similarly aged thirty-three-year-old daughter, Antonia. Cecy decided to go back to her parents' house in Panama while I tried to find a position.

After two more months of no interviews, my time was running out. Antonia was moving into a new apartment unit, and I no longer wanted to be a burden to her and her roommate. I stayed to help Antonia move all of her furniture up the stairs to the third floor and returned to Panama to be with my family.

Chapter 46

"Why don't you go to Costa Rica and throw out the renter so we can open our own business?" Cecy's words were firm and engulfed in anger.

I looked into my wife's eyes and knew I had to be delicate with my answer. Cecy did not know Jaco; to me, Jaco was the devil's backyard, his playground with all of his toys. I had consistently fought so many different sides and levels of my life's corruption: I had lost or destroyed a twenty-two-year marriage and fathered a beautiful bastard son as I failed to put the final seal on his mother's engagement ring. My Jaco life had turned me into a semi-paranoid hermit who spent his time waving at working girls and greeting his front-door security squad of transvestites who worked off his patio. All I wanted to do was avoid Jaco at all costs.

"Cecy, you don't know Jaco; it has destroyed everything I have ever built in my life, and it will destroy us," I said. "I don't want to go back there."

Cecy looked at me. She was very angry. "You're just lazy; you don't want to work."

"It's not that, baby," I responded firmly. "I don't mind working. I've worked since I was five. I just don't want anything to hurt this family; I love you and Lucy too much."

She was half right, but a lazy man doesn't play tennis six times a week and work out at the gym when the money is good. Cecy was done talking to me and walked away.

I contemplated my options for a few days. I knew I didn't have much of a choice. My rational mind was right in knowing that Jaco could never be good for us, but my heart wanted to prove to my wife that I wasn't lazy, that I knew how to create great businesses, and that liquor life in Jaco was dangerous. Since Cecy didn't drink, I thought I had a fighting chance.

Joey's family was continuing to not pay any rent, and our funds just kept going south. I got my lawyer on the phone, and we made a plan to evict the tenant. It was going to take a few months to evict them. My family and I decided to return to Costa Rica to keep a close eye on the proceedings.

My ex-wife, Joanna, was generous enough to let us stay in the house we had purchased on the mountains in Escazu—at least until she got a tenant. Joanna had been happy to have us stay in her house for a couple of days, mainly because it was an opportunity for her to become close with her stepdaughter, Lucy. Lucy had a special magic with everyone who came into contact with her. I knew my little girl was very pretty with her wonderful curly Afro and adorable smile, but she brought something else within her spirit that made everyone who came within a certain distance of her attracted to her like a magnet.

Staying at the Escazu house was actually nice for me as well. I appreciated once again having the beautiful view of *las Montañas de las Brujas* (the mountains of the Witches). I used to come home from the restaurant after closing Valle Azul, grab a Cognac, smoke a Cuban Cohiba cigar, and enjoy the dead silence that huddled in the darkness of the valley before bed.

I could see in Cecy's eyes that she was struggling to be happy. Our world was crumbling around us, and we had one shot left to save whatever was left of our finances and us. Cecy and I had both come from worlds of deprivation. When one starts at deprivation, grows far from it, and then falls back down to it, the sense of deprivation doubles. My job at this point was to stay as calm as possible and try not to feed into the slowly developing nightmare of my family's destruction.

Chapter 47

AS I'D LEARNED THUS FAR DURING MY TIME IN COSTA RICA, THERE IS one thing that completely dominates the Tico mind and culture, and it's fútbol. Not USA "football," but the football that is treasured everywhere in the world and called "soccer" in North America.

We happened to be going through the eviction process with the tenants of the Fusion building during the World Cup, and Costa Rica just happened to have a world-class team competing that year. If one wanted to see an entire country stop in their tracks, all they'd need to do is be in Costa Rica when they play in the World Cup, or when the rival teams "Saprissa" and "La Liga" play each other.

It just so happened that in the year 2014, Costa Rica's team "selection" was showing the world that their very small country could compete with the best teams in the world. The Costa Rica Selection played their way all the way to the quarterfinals. They even beat Germany. It was one of the most magical times in our lives as we watched every man, woman, and child celebrating each win on every street patio and rooftop. I'd never witnessed an entire country come together as one. We could not help but bathe in the Ticos' joy.

Chapter 48

THE TICOS LOST TO THE NETHERLANDS IN THE WORLD CUP quarterfinals, and we lost the place we were staying in. Joanna had found a tenant, and we needed to find a cheap place to stay. My best man Raymond's friend Rosemary had bought his house from him. The house was located farther up the mountain. It had a wooden cabin behind it that had housed Raymond's property mate, David. She was willing to rent it to us at the affordable price of three hundred dollars per month. The price was right, the house was beautiful and comfortable, and Rosemary had pleasingly enhanced Raymond's beautiful garden. Cecy and I thought we were about to live in our own little piece of paradise as we walked to our nature-surrounded cabin through the wild and colorful flora of the Costa Rican mountains.

"Oh my god!" I felt the words leave my mouth as soon as I walked into the cabin. I instantly lost every single shred of respect I'd had for David. I would think that a financially stable, old, and sick gringo would set up something nice for his final years. David's cabin turned Herman's little infested house by the restaurant into a picture for *Architectural Digest*. The size of the cockroaches competed with the size of the mice. There were flying and dancing tiny insects absolutely everywhere.

Cecy and I went to war with the cabin; we sprayed, poisoned, and put aerosol bombs in the cabin for two days. After the chemical warfare, we washed everything with bleach. We were not being environmentally sensitive—we were going broke, had lost our home, and were carrying huge attitudes on our shoulders—and we just wanted to sleep in peace.

When the cabin was finally suitable for healthy humans, we moved in. We found out the first night at the cabin that it would practically get cold enough to snow every night because of the altitude. I started religiously bringing wood into the cabin and lighting the woodburning stove every single day. Our neighbor, a friend of Herman, had a family of rottweilers that enjoyed watching us and looking for opportunities to get revenge for the time I had protected my rights and properties from Herman. Needless to say, I had an automatic enemy.

The great thing about living in the Costa Rica Mountains was that the majority of the people who lived in the mountains were amazing, especially if you could speak Spanish. The Ticos on the mountain had not changed what they did and how they lived for hundreds of years. Most of them had coffee or cattle farms. Their most precious possessions were their prized oxen and the beautifully hand-painted carts they paraded around the town during specific holidays.

There was a bus that came close to the cabin, but we would have to climb the fifty-five-degree slanted street for three hundred yards to our cabin. For exercise, I would sometimes walk up and down the entire mountain. The Ticos on the mountain knew what I'd done to the restaurant Valle Azul. I used to run up and down the hill with my car, but now that I walked, I could communicate with them, and it made me and them very happy. They gave me a lot of respect and friendship all along the mountain slope.

Our monthly rental at the cabin did not last more than thirty days. One day, Cecy went outside to check on Lucy and found her looking at four rottweilers that had jumped the fence. Cecy pulled Lucy into the house, and I confronted the dogs. I knew I could not show any fear. I picked up the nearest piece of wood, held it down by my hip, and looked the dogs in the eyes. I did not want to provoke them, but I wanted to show them that I was the alpha of my home.

To my lucky relief and surprise, Rosemary's dog came outside to cover my back. The yelling and the barking could have won an Oscar for "best display of machismo." The rottweilers finally decided that the whole scene of the big black man with Lassie was too confusing for Tico Mountain dogs and left.

Cecy and I expressed our concerns to Rosemary, but she seemed powerless to control the Tico neighbor, whose family had been in the mountains for generations. My family had to live in fear every day as we returned home. If I wasn't there, Cecy and Lucy never left the house. When I was there, I would sit outside like a security guard as Lucy played outside in the beautiful gardens.

It was very difficult for us to avoid Joanna and her delicious food since we lived so close to her. She was one of the best eclectic gourmet chefs in Costa Rica, and we could not resist going to her converted house to eat at her private restaurant. Everything was fine and friendly with Joanna and my family as long as we had money in our pockets. Joanna's "Camp Florence Kid's Magic" continued to work on Lucy as they fell in love with each other.

After three months of actually enjoying what seemed to be a typical Tico life, my cell phone rang.

"Tony, it's done," Adrian, my lawyer, said.

"You're kidding me! I can evict them?" I asked in pure joy.

"Yes!" said Adrian. "All the arrangements are being made with the police. Tomorrow we'll go in with the police to evict them and make sure they don't take anything out of the restaurant. They didn't pay, so the judge also awarded you everything inside the restaurant."

"I can't believe it," I replied. "Thank you, Adrian. Great job. I will see you tomorrow."

Cecy was ecstatic, and we thought that our suffering was finally over. We had the building back, and we also had all the equipment needed to run a functional restaurant inside. We decided to live in the small apartment I had built in the restaurant for the live bands who used to play at Fusion. It had a bathroom and a shower, which was sufficient for a family who was going to eat from the kitchen of the restaurant.

We made a deal to break the lease with Rosemary, packed up the little we had left, and proceeded to Jaco to reclaim our pride. Deep down inside, I could foresee the destruction Jaco would wreak upon my life, yet I was so blindly in love with Cecy that I led myself to believe that everything was going to be all right and that our relationship was so strong that it could withstand the wrath of Jaco. Cecy was not like my first wife, Joanna, who'd fed me to the wolves in order to be with my waiter; she had a strong and righteous family base that would hold her and our family together through all negative and sometimes deadly challenges from the "Jaco Reaper."

I felt a little bit like a Nazi when my lawyer and the Jaco police force entered my restaurant. I sat next to whom I thought was the manager as the police spread out to guard each area of the restaurant. If there was one thing Jaco police knew, it was how to facilitate an eviction.

"What the hell is going on here?" the obviously gringo owner and manager asked me in total surprise.

"This is an eviction," I replied. "My name is Tony, and I am the owner of the property. I don't know who you are, but Paul has not paid the rent. I am taking back the bar and everything in it to cover the rent."

This guy then realized the seriousness of the situation and quickly switched to business-survival mode. "Hi, my name is Anthony," he said in a warm tone. "Do they call you Anthony too?" he asked while shaking my hand. "I am one of the partners Paul has told you about. The reason I am here is to take over the business. Paul was spending the profits on drugs and working girls. That is why you didn't get paid."

Anthony didn't have to tell me twice; I had seen many businesses and people fall down what I called the black hole because they'd gotten sucked into the sordid life of Jaco. If one wanted to walk through the valley of temptation, they'd bring their tightrope to Jaco.

I was able to empathize with Anthony's dilemma. I also didn't want any problems with a group of New York Italians who owned a fleet of fishing yachts. "Anthony, I understand what happens here, but I'm out a lot of rent money—not to exclude the money I had to spend on the lawyers during this process."

Anthony didn't hesitate before replying, "Tony, I know we are behind in the rent, and I will make everything up to you and more. As you can see, we put a lot into this business and would like to stay here. I promise we will be on time with the rent from now on."

I knew how much restaurant and entertainment equipment cost. I noticed as soon as I'd walked in that the kitchen was complete, the bar was a bartender's wet dream, the tables were made of strong wood, and the professional audio equipment set up in the corner of the restaurant had to be worth around $15,000.

I ran through the numbers as we spoke; the rent was $1,500 per month. My high-interest loan monthly payments were $1,500 per month. I had about $30,000 in the bank after refinancing. My business instincts told me to make a deal with this man and get myself and my family the hell out of Jaco, but my love for Cecy and desire to prove she was wrong about me being lazy compelled me to push Anthony out the door with his accounting books.

Anthony's final words to me were: "Tony, take some time to think about it."

The word hit the streets as soon as Anthony closed the door behind him: "Tony's back with his new wife, and they are going to reopen Fusion."

I spent a lot of time once again planning a new concept for a restaurant in Jaco. My expertise was coming up with concepts that were missing from Jaco, that would fill a hole in its selection of options, and that had a high probability of being successful there. The people in Jaco had been conditioned to think: *No working girls, no bar!* Yet that was far from the truth. The hotels and the town of Jaco housed many people who would not go out at night because they felt uncomfortable with the environment. Joanna and I had provided a place for those non-hooker-type people to feel secure when we opened Onyx. I knew I could do it again.

Cecy and I decided to open a first-class diner that hosted Costa Rican cultural dance shows. It was time for the Ticos to show their amazing and colorful culture, which was being hidden from the tourists and from the Ticos themselves in and around Jaco. When it came to the working girls, we would have the same policy as I'd had at Onyx; they would only be able to come one at a time and with a date. It wasn't that I was against working girls; I was going after a certain customer base, and I was not going to let anything interfere with my business concept.

Chapter 49

I WAS PUSHING MY SPIRIT TO BE POSITIVE AND AT THE SAME TIME ACCEPT the reality of our situation. Deep down inside, I worried about the future of my family. The wonderful part of my return to Jaco was being around my son, Nico, who was growing into a solid young man and was easily accessible for the many hugs he loved to give his second family. I tried to build a visual mental fence around my family to defend us from what always inevitably creeps in through the cracks of expatriate lives in Jaco. I hadn't been prepared for the struggles of maintaining a relationship in Jaco the first two times I'd tried, but this time, I thought I was. I thought my experience in Jaco thus far would now be my cornerstone of survival for myself, my new and naïve wife, and our relationship.

Cecy had proven over and over again that she loved me and would protect my heart. I trusted her more than I trusted myself. I wanted to be her hero, and I was taking the chance of showing her what I could do—even if it meant doing it in the devil's backyard.

Chapter 50

THE CHANGING-ROOM APARTMENT IN THE BACK OF THE RESTAURANT was too small for the three of us, but we made makeshift beds on the floor of the restaurant with the bench cushions that our customers sat on during opening hours. We had a business plan; it was very well thought out. Cecy, being the expert on Central American culture, knew exactly what she needed to do in order to orchestrate a traditional dance presentation. She researched and found the perfect dance company to hire. We drove to Orotina and made a deal with the manager of the dance company she'd chosen. Our roommate, Mark Art, slept in the storage room of the restaurant and designed and painted the new Fusion interior and exterior look. Nico's mother, Nuria, designed the posters and brochures advertising the new Fusion and the traditional dance shows. I sold my reputation as a business owner who created prostitution-free environments to the biggest hotels in the area to get on their lists of safe places to go for tourists. Everyone in Jaco knew me and my reputation; the hotels and restaurant owners jumped cautiously on board.

We made a deal with who we thought was one of the best chefs in Jaco. Cecy and I had discovered this extremely creative Tico chef by going out and sampling reputable restaurants in Jaco at random. Rodolfo had had a little bit of training outside of the country. He felt he was at least ten steps above the rest, especially since he'd gotten his international training in Italy. Italian and French cuisine dominated the Tico restaurant culture. The general Tico population gave extra credit to restaurants that were able to deliver quality French and Italian foods in addition to traditional Tico meals. If they couldn't deliver a decent variety of traditional Tico meals, restaurants wouldn't see business from the locals, the tourists they met, or their friends ever again. Rodolfo was able to do both international and traditional Tico cuisines.

I insisted on including a typical Tico menu consisting of *casados* (rice, beans, and eggs served with beef, fish, or pork), *costillas* (spareribs with all the fat), and *platos mixtos* (a family plate combination of *chicharrones*, *costillas* and *plátanos* (plantains). I knew the trials and tribulations I had to deal with in serving the Tico cuisine—the vegetables were always fresh, and the spices had to be right on—but the pork was extra greasy, and the Tico cow meat made every dentist wealthy. The new generation of much more tender cow was moving in and was now available through the major distributors and local butchers. The order had to be very specific when ordering cuts like New York or Rib Eye. The new Fusion would only serve our customers the best before they were mesmerized by the colorful and beautiful three-hundred-year culture of the traditional Tico dancers.

Hotels and businesses that catered to tourists knew my reputation for keeping a comfortable environment for tourists in Jaco. I met with them again to confirm that I was going forward with the same family-oriented business concept, and I let them know I was now taking it to another level by introducing their tourist guests to real Tico culture with the entertainment provided at Fusion. Most tourists had no idea how real and beautiful the real Tico culture was; they only scratched the surface with the birds, beaches, and volcanos. Jaco consistently missed out on the true beauty and tradition of the family-friendly sides of Tico culture, and I wanted to present it to the world.

We were very excited about our opening as we lined up seats every night to support the bench cushions that would complete our makeshift beds. The makeshift beds were very uncomfortable, but we made the best of it. We had no choice but to live in the restaurant; we couldn't afford anything else. At least the restaurant had a bathroom, a sink, and a cold-water shower. I think survival mode was actually becoming our way of life.

The new Fusion had only been open for less than thirty days when I returned to the restaurant from making my monthly payment on my high-interest bridge loan to find a multitude of policemen around the restaurant and many people in the streets. *Wow! A parade right by our restaurant; this is great advertisement,* I thought. At that point, I thought the police were there for crowd control, and I was very happy that Fusion was getting a high level of exposure. I parked in front of the restaurant and walked the few steps to the restaurant; when I turned the corner of the patio that led to the entrance, I saw my wife between two policemen. She was crying, shaking from head to toe, and bouncing rapidly up and down.

"What the hell is going on here?" The words came automatically out of my mouth.

Cecy tried to compose herself as she looked me directly in the eye. "A man who was a serial killer came for happy hour. He was acting very strangely." My wife needed to breathe and collect herself again; she never moved from her position between the two policemen. "The police were able to signal to us to get out of the bar, so we went to the kitchen to act like we were going to cook. When the police entered, he reached for his gun, they shot him. I had Lucy and the kids behind the cement wall in the kitchen."

"Where's Lucy?" I didn't care if there was fire raining from the sky; Lucy was all I was concerned about.

"She's across the street with Paola," Cecy automatically responded.

I ran over to hug my baby girl, relieved that my family was still complete.

I watched the lucky criminal struggle for his life on the stretcher as they carried his bleeding body out of our restaurant and apartment. I entered and watched a brave waitress take a cloth, dip it in the puddle of blood, and wring the flow into a bucket over and over again. Depression engulfed my mind; I had lived in Costa Rica long enough to have a fairly deep understanding of their culture. The memory of a conversation I had with my ex-Valle Azul manager Tabo appeared in my mind. As Tabo and I had passed a restaurant on route to a shop in Santa Ana one day, Tabo shared with me the story of a murder that had taken place at that restaurant, leaving bloodstains all over the walls. Tabo had told me that after the murder, not one single Tico would step a foot in that restaurant. I knew deep inside I was given an omen. I was not superstitious, but I'd thought the spirit of Costa Rica still loved me and what I'd done for her. I had just kept pushing her advice aside to prove something to my young and naïve wife.

The grand opening of the new Fusion was held a few weeks after we opened—and after the murderer incident—and it boasted great food and service and the beautiful and colorful "Typical Tico Dancers." They were expensive, but they put on a first-class professional show. Only gringo tourists attended, but they were absolutely delighted.

The new Fusion had a great concept. The word spread quickly. The Marriott Los Suenos, Villas Caletas, and all the Jaco five-star hotels were ready to come aboard the Fusion ship. The dancers were worth it, but the balance sheet was tilting rapidly toward the red. I wasn't in the dark; I knew it would take some time to fill enough tables to make a profit. Fusion was running on my last savings from the high-interest loan, my mother's life savings, and borrowed money. I wasn't too worried; I had taken out a loan from the bank a few years back, and it had been paid on time. My plan was to refinance the high-interest bridge loan through the normal banking system at half the interest rate the private loaner was charging me. The plan was to increase our bank loan enough to have a six-month cash flow and pay back my mother and everyone else who had supported me through our struggles.

Chapter 51

"WHAT DO YOU MEAN I OWE THE BANK OVER $100,000?" I ASKED THE loan officer at Banco Nacional. I'd had no doubts in my mind when I'd gone to the Banco Nacional. I had taken a loan out on the white building with the Banco Nacional, paid the monthly payments on time, and sold the property to Daystar with a contractual agreement that Daystar would pay off the mortgage. Seven years had passed, but somehow the more than $100,000 mortgage still existed—and under my company's name. It was too late; the banker had given Cecy the bank's mortgage statement before she'd had a chance to think about the illegalities of the situation. Everyone involved with the sale and the mortgage knew something was very wrong; in the States, this would have been a clear breach of contract, and a settlement would have been made or the property would have been returned to me instantly. Every lawyer we spoke to in Costa Rica said the legal process there would take time and cost at least twelve thousand dollars. I had the challenge of trying to make enough profit in sixty days to buy another sixty days and another sixty days to survive without a bank loan. I was holding onto the side of the boat, hoping the sharks that constantly surrounded and fed on us would somehow have their fill before we reached high season.

The sharks reached me well before high season creeped into Costa Rica. The braille of the demise of our lives and business began to penetrate the walls of the restaurant. Cost elimination was a daily priority. The first to go were the dancers, and then Cecy and I took the place of the waiters and bartenders. Finally, we had to part ways with Rodolfo the chef.

Closure was inevitable; no matter how hard Cecy and I tried to hold up the roof of our dream, we had to close. Through the disaster, I actually started to admire my wife's fortitude and the diligence she applied in her efforts to avoid failure. Cecy went into high gear, collecting text and evidence from the bank.

Pat was the president of Daystar Properties; I knew him, and he knew me. Pat knew I had a solid reputation in Jaco, and he didn't want his name dragged through the dirt. I called him, and we set up a meeting.

My therapist had once told me a parable when I lived in New York that illustrated how a snake will always be a snake—and Pat was the epitome of that story. Pat's office was where my apartment used to be on the third floor of what was now Daystar's headquarters. Seven years ago, upon hearing that I had been planning to sell the building to a hooker bar, Pat had sent two of his men, one of whom was one of my tennis partners, to make a convenient cash counteroffer I couldn't resist. We'd signed the contract with the condition that Daystar would pay off the mortgage on the building the day we signed the contract. Seven years had passed, and my livelihood was being destroyed because I still had my company name on the unpaid loan.

"Hello, Tony. Nice to see you," Pat said as Cecy and I stepped into his office. "This must be your lovely wife."

I personally didn't want any friction, yet Cecy, being the hot-blooded Panamanian she was, had a different attitude.

I got right to the point. "Pat, what the fuck? Why wasn't this loan paid off—and how were you able to keep my name on the loan in the bank? I'm getting hurt here. I had to close my business."

Pat pretended he was listening, waited a couple of seconds, and said the last words I wanted to hear: "Tony, we had no idea you were going to return to Costa Rica. The loan payments are being made on time, so there's no problem there. Don't worry; we will take care of it."

I wondered why Pat's company didn't handle this transaction with integrity; they had hundreds of high-end condominiums. The small property they'd bought from me should have been paid for by their penny jar. While talking to Pat, an idea developed in my mind that Daystar's financial position may actually have been dancing around over-expenditures or even bankruptcy. Pat and his group were from California, and I knew the North American business mind; when US businessmen were stressed, they'd look for any excuse to not cooperate. I felt like I needed to tread carefully. Cecy wanted Pat's head on a stick. I wanted the same thing as my wife, but I had to leave every door open to find a solution. If Pat bailed on me, Fusion and my family were finished financially.

My lawyer was also a friend and part of the same social network I was in, and he knew I was broke. Adrian was not independent; he worked for RE&B *Abagados* (Lawyers), which was one of the best law firms in Costa

Rica. Even though I'd been a high-paying client in the past, business was business. The other Tico lawyers wanted huge fees to prosecute Daystar over months, if not years, in this case where the breach of contract was so obvious.

Cecy and I were now selling the restaurant's televisions to feed our family.

Chapter 52

"TONY, I'M GOING TO HELP YOU OUT, MY FRIEND," RICO, MY PRIVATE LOAN administrator, said to me when I met him at the Beetle Bar to refinance my loan. Rico had been the ringmaster of securing us a bridge loan, which had an interest rate 80 percent higher than our existing bridge loan. He knew our desperate timeline, and I'm sure he capitalized well on the transaction.

Rico was a black Tico; most black Ticos came from the Caribbean Atlantic side of Costa Rica. From what I heard, they were contained on the Atlantic side until the early 1960s. Limón was the main city in the containment area and became quite dangerous at night. Puerto Viejo, another town situated an hour south of Limón on the Caribbean side, had beautiful beaches and still maintained the wonderfully rich culture, food, and music of the "Negros" (Black People) or "*Morenos*" (Mulattos).

Rico had spent enough time with his relocated parents in the States to have a very good understanding of how to manipulate both Tico and North American cultures. He had been introduced to me by "Dave the Dude" at Valle Azul as one of the richest men in Costa Rica, and I'm sure it wasn't just me who found out why.

Rico continued his presentation to my desperation. "The owner of one of the most successful Caribbean restaurants in Limón wants to rent Fusion," he said.

I really had no choice but to continue listening.

"Tony, he has the money and the know-how to make a great restaurant. There doesn't yet exist a Caribbean restaurant close to Jaco Beach or the Manuel Antonia Beach, which is located forty minutes south of Jaco. He's famous throughout the Caribbean community. I guarantee he will pay on time."

I decided to play along with Rico's presentation and just throw out a number. "I have the loan, and I need a place to live and take care of my family. I want $2,500 per month, a one-month security deposit, and an option out if I sell the property." I thought Rico would walk away, leaving me to continue with my "doctorate" in survival.

Rico hesitated for a second; he knew my situation. I was not going to consider anything less than the money I felt I needed in order to buy time to sell the property and take decent care of my family.

Rico returned to Jaco a few days later with Olman, the very successful Atlantic-coast Caribbean-food restaurant owner. Olman walked into Fusion like he was gliding on ice, seeing that the restaurant was still ready to function.

Cecy, Rico, Olman, and I sat at one of the tables at the front of the restaurant. I picked the table on purpose so that Olman would be in prime positioning to keep viewing the possibilities.

I got myself mentally prepared for some level of negotiation. Olman looked at me, bobbing his head up and down. "So, $2,500?" he said smoothly with his deep Caribbean accent.

"Yes, and not one penny lower," I replied very confidently. The only way I'd have a chance to breathe without a respirator was at that price. Otherwise, I'd continue my quest to sell that property as fast as possible. Low season had set in, and no one was buying anything in Jaco. The prices had shot through the roof, and every shrewd buyer was going to wait for the crash. The problem was that Fusion had a stigma of failure and bad luck. I knew the killer and the gunfight had caused a superstition Ticos had secretly gossiped about throughout the entire country. Just like the drums of Africa or the smoke of the American Indians, Costa Rica's word of mouth is one of the most powerful cultural traditions one can witness.

"OK, I'm good with that," Olman responded, continuing to bob his head up and down.

Personally, I was a little shocked. *Maybe Rico did help me out this time.* I'd done some homework, and his restaurant was very popular.

"OK, it's a deal," I said. "I'll have my lawyer make the contract, and we can sign it as soon as it's ready."

We shook hands, he left, and Cecy and I hugged. I thought, *I haven't lost. I still have a chance to save my property, which is all I have left. I needed extra time to sell the property, and I got it.* I was so tired of living on the edge of desperation and fear, and I just wanted to take my family to the States and start a new life.

We got lucky and found a cute little house in Escazu at an affordable price, close enough to the center of the town for us to walk there. Cecy was quite happy with having a home in which she could entertain our small group of friends. The owner worked for an American corporation and had put a North American touch in the construction of his house—and all the utilities worked properly during our stay. I didn't really understand the Tico way of thinking when it came to tiny insects because we once again had to fumigate the entire house before we moved in.

Our lives when we were in Escazu were comfortable. I once again started frequenting the Bella Horizonte Tennis Club, which I'd discovered the first year I'd moved to Costa Rica; it was, as always, the perfect place to relax. Cecy enjoyed watching my skills toggle between the beginner and intermediate levels. Lucy was still at an age that allowed her to enjoy feeling important in her role of chasing down the tennis balls and throwing them back to the server. The Bella Horizonte Tennis Club had many rough edges in its courts, but it was my serenity from all that I had to endure and the weight of the stress I entertained in my soul. Raymond and I would play tennis, eat lunch, and down cocktails as we tried to solve every riddle of the universe.

Cecy and I continued to meet with Daystar, and it seemed like Pat had an incontinent bull in his mouth. I couldn't understand why a company that had purchased some of the most expensive properties at Jaco Beach and built hundreds of luxury condominiums couldn't honorably pay a measly $100,000 mortgage.

The property Fusion was on was one thousand square meters and was located one hundred meters from the ocean. The real estate market in Costa Rica had crashed because of the growing crime rate. Real estate became a lot more expensive than its actual value, and every smart investor knew it was a buyer's market. People just waited to buy properties that failed or were repossessed by lenders. Fusion had a bad reputation because of the flooding that used to occur during the rainy season, let alone the murderer drama. I had fixed the first problem by sending some very brave young men from Nicaragua to battle with the bats who had resided under Fusion and clear the clogging in the drains that had been caused by the floods, but there was no fix for the word that had spread about the gunfight.

Only three months after Olman began renting the restaurant from me, he failed to pay the rent on time. "Baby, Olman hasn't paid the rent," I told Cecy. This time, I was actually surprised. I'd thought Olman was the "real

McCoy;" I'd checked him out through people I knew. I didn't trust Rico anymore, but Olman and his family seemed genuine.

"*Yo no creo*" (I don't believe it), Cecy replied in Spanish. "This is bullshit."

We left for Jaco the next day to meet with Olman.

My guardian angels had shown me a lot of love through the bulk of my life; I felt special when they took me out of the ghetto and sent me to the other side. My angels had helped me wiggle out of many awkward situations as I massaged my mind to absorb the racial innuendoes, rejections, and extreme levels of insecurity I'd experienced. They'd held my head up high and painted a face of confidence over my real one, so I could endure, and many times become the "Great Pretender." I was starting to think that I had angered my angels. I methodically picked through my actions in Costa Rica to pinpoint which one had put me out of their grace. I wanted to apologize and pray for forgiveness. I knew a black hole was gradually opening for me; I had used to joke about it in other people's lives, but now my name was engraved on it.

Chapter 53

OLMAN AND RICO WERE WAITING FOR US WHEN WE OPENED FUSION'S door. Cecy put on her game face. My wife and I were both tired of trusting that at least one legal contract would be honored, yet again, I remained calm. I had been taught a long time ago by Joanna's father that when one negotiates, one should never twist someone's arm; they should do their homework to be prepared to know what they are talking about and gain respect from the other party.

"What's up?" I asked, cutting straight to the point, "I was told I was not going to have to worry about our agreement." I stayed very calm.

Olman and Rico knew they'd pitched the hell out of me on how Olman was solid and would pay on time every month. I was also being careful because I knew that my financial position was sitting on top of a wall that would have impressed Humpty Dumpty. If Olman failed, so did I.

Rico was quiet; he knew he was definitely not the one I wanted to hear. Olman took the stage and said, "Tony, I told you about the loan I was waiting for from the bank. It's taking longer than I thought."

I was listening to him, but my mind was giving me another presentation at the same time: *If this guy has such a successful restaurant in Limón, it would not even be a thought for his bank to help him franchise his business. What is the real problem? Rico may have had extensive training in the States, but he's Tico. When you insult a Tico like Brian did with the hotel owner back in the Onyx days, they will not only fire back—they will use a bazooka.* I started to reach back through my memory, double-checking each time I had spoken to or spent time with Rico. Had I ever given him a symbolic middle finger?

Deep down, I felt Olman was a stand-up guy. I think he was manipulated into thinking he could pull off another franchise way before it was time. "When do you think your loan will be approved?" I asked, giving Olman the signal that I wanted to work with him. I profoundly understood the fact that we needed him more than he needed me. I could see that he wanted to do the right thing, yet the reality was that Olman was not in the secure financial position he'd presumed he was in.

"The bank said the loan should be ready next week," Olman replied, buying time.

I had no choice but to donate faith to his quest. I had a $1,500 per month loan on the property. Every Realtor knew I was desperate to sell, but the real estate market was dead, and I'm sure all of their clients were told to wait. I lowered the price of the property from the $800,000 it had been for the past three years, to $400,000, and received not one single bid. Daystar knew I wasn't financially sound enough to bring them to court. The higher-ups must have had a great chuckle about it at their business dinners.

"OK, Olman! I really think you mean well," I said. "I'm going to work with you for now, but if this situation drags on into next month, you have to promise me you'll leave without any problems." Even though Olman had cash flow problems, I still thought he had integrity.

"I promise, Tony," he replied. "I will have the money next week."

I left that meeting as stressed as I'd been when I'd arrived. My wife had wanted me to be strong and twist their arms, yet that wasn't an option; one can't squeeze an orange out of a seed. Cecy and I returned to our little house in Escazu with many doubts.

No matter how hard my family tried to have a decent life, we just weren't allowed. Once again, our finances were labeled code red, and food shopping had very strict limitations. I tried to hide the shame and helplessness that burned inside my soul; here was the little boy who had been put on a cultural rocket ship, eaten at the finest restaurants in New York, and forged his way through the Serengeti, only to find himself yet again rationing his food budget. I'd been a fucking regional manager with a company car, $30,000 expense account, and a house on an acre in Westchester County, New York. Now I would get stressed if my little girl chose something special for herself that was not on the shopping list. I woke up every day afraid Cecy would say, "Tony, Lucy and I are going back to Panama."

As the church bells tolled every hour, each day, for a week and then a month, Olman never paid. Olman's excuses started to sound like an echo during the second month. I called my lawyer, and he set up a meeting with Olman, Cecy, and myself. My lawyer explained to Olman his options, and I consistently reminded Olman of his promise to leave without a problem. Everyone agreed to a time frame, and Cecy and I got ready to go back into business at Fusion. Our debts were piling up. I made a deal for breaking the lease with the owner of the house we'd been living in, packed up the little bit of stuff we had left, and proceeded to Jaco to reclaim our pride.

Olman was waiting at Fusion to hand us the keys and left promptly with his family, heading back to Limón. Cecy and I each had a copy of the inventory list and proceeded to check for every item we'd left for Olman to operate his business. We were pleasantly surprised to find everything in order and discover that Olman had left the restaurant stocked with enough food, beer, and liquor for us to make a plan to reopen the restaurant.

My nomad family once again started the process of cleaning our home to our specifications. We looked forward to seeing our gentrified circle of friends that we'd connected with during our sporadic appearances as restaurant owners in Jaco.

Mark Art was the first to enter the door; Mark had lived with us when he first came to conquer Jaco. Mark came from Florida carrying past-life secrets equal to those of the majority of the people who immigrated to Costa Rica from another country. What impressed me and stood out the most about Mark was the fact that he was an amazing mural artist. He enhanced the entrance of Fusion, and we paid Mark with a dormitory room and a hell of a lot of beer. I had no idea how much beer Mark could drink; I should have paid him in cash or gold bullion.

There is something smooth, charming, and devilish about people who live by and drink the fresh Caribbean water. One day, a black man around forty years old glided into my restaurant with a very serious dark-skinned young woman. I could tell he'd done his homework; just by watching him lock in on me, I knew that he knew exactly who I was. My businesses in Costa Rica had created exposure for me throughout their society for fifteen years. I saw how the waiters whispered about me in every restaurant or bar I attended. Joanna and I were famous from the Atlantic coast of Costa Rica to the Pacific.

"Hey, boss, can we speak with you?" the smooth Caribbean man confidently blurted out as he waved me over in order to make his woman think he had power over the situation.

I slowly walked to the side of the bar where the man and his lady had planted themselves. I recognized the woman; she had been Olman's second chef.

"Hey, boss—"

"Call me Tony," I interrupted. "What's your name?" I put my hand out to shake his. I'd interrupted him because I didn't want to be patronized; if there was one thing I was learning the hard way about living in Costa Rica, it was to be firm but humble.

"Harold," he replied. "Tony, my woman was the cook here, and Olman owes her a lot of money."

I didn't doubt his words for one second.

"She's behind on her rent and needs a job. She may have been the second cook, but she was a better cook than the first—and she can prove it to you."

"What is your name?" I asked the woman; she had obviously accepted the typical woman's role in a clearly male-dominated culture.

"Jasmin," she said softly, being careful not to lose her place with Harold, but giving subtle indications that she wasn't as submissive as he thought she was.

"Nice to meet you, Jasmin," I responded. "Do you feel comfortable cooking everything on the menu?" I had no time to waste; I needed a working business as soon as possible. I needed her, and she needed me.

"Yes," Jasmin said without hesitation.

"I can only pay you what Olman was paying you," I said. I didn't want to insult Jasmin, but I knew Ticos paid their employees in the service industry much less than gringos did. I knew I probably didn't have a chance in hell to survive without Daystar freeing my mortgage, but I had to try; I was out of options.

"Is that OK with you, baby?" Harold asked his woman.

"Yes, I need to work," Jasmin replied promptly. She was also out of options, especially since Harold was a musician in the small country of Costa Rica.

I looked at Harold to make sure he was in agreement. "OK, Jasmin, the kitchen's yours."

We had enough product to at least try to create a cash flow. Cecy and I were actually loving the fact that we were reopening a Caribbean restaurant connected to both of our African cultures. Harold appreciated us hiring his woman, and he would use his music and equipment on the patio to draw attention to the new Fusion Caribbean Restaurant and Bar.

Revamping the Caribbean restaurant for the people of Jaco to enjoy wasn't enough to keep the restaurant afloat; low season was drawing near, and there weren't many tourists. Some of Olman's Atlantic coast customers came to see if we served authentic Caribbean food as well and were pleasantly surprised that Jasmin made authentic Caribbean food that exceeded their expectations. Personally, I thought I had a handle on Caribbean food until I tasted the true Caribbean rice and beans. The real Caribbean rice and beans was better than ice cream.

The business at Fusion was minimal to none throughout the low season; we took a loss every day. This time, the big hotels hesitated to recommend Fusion to their customers because of our inconsistencies. The trickle of customers we did get actually enjoyed the food, service, and attention they received from Cecy and me. When high season once again approached us, I knew we had to create something to make the local people comfortable with bringing the tourists with them to Fusion. We knew a woman named Ginger who had a reputation throughout Jaco as a good and faithful waitress, and she was also one of the best karaoke presenters in the town. She agreed to be a waitress and present karaoke two nights a week at Fusion.

One day, as I was working, I pointed out to a nurse, one of the few regulars at Fusion, that the skin on my hands and feet was turning hard and black. She didn't say anything, and she didn't have to; her expression said all that I needed to hear. I was falling ill to one of the Central American jungle's mysterious illnesses while trying to survive a financial crisis. I had no time or money to spare for a doctor's appointment—even though I knew I needed one.

Our valiant effort was not enough to get Fusion off the ground. It took less than three months of borrowing from the bare minimum of trust I had left to deplete our funds and our spirits. Cecy and I were putting as much pressure on Daystar as we could without a lawyer. They had some of the biggest enemies and the best lawyers in Costa Rica. Pat, the president of Daystar, who now felt he was the "Teflon Don" of Jaco Beach, knew we were basically powerless when it came to putting legal pressure on him or Daystar; he knew he didn't have to do the right thing.

My family became disparity's best friend. We tried to make deals with the local lawyers to no avail; they performed as if they were going to help us, but they never made one move on their laptops. We put "televisions for sale" signs on the outdoor whiteboard, knowing that selling our televisions would be the most efficient way to keep food on our table.

My skin was continuing to get dark and form hard islands all over my body. The hard spots were slowly but surely spreading from my feet and hands up to my buttocks, chest, and neck, and desperation and the vanity of protecting my face drove me to make an appointment with a dermatologist in San José. I felt guilty spending some of our food money on myself, but I was becoming very worried that I had something that was eating me from the inside out.

When I arrived at the dermatologist's sixties-fashioned office, I began to have flashbacks of the time Joanna had gone to a doctor in Escazu for the removal of pins left in her foot from the bunion surgery she'd had in New York. It was dusk in Escazu center when we'd found the office of the local general practitioner recommended to Joanna by our cleaning woman. The office was completely unsanitary, and the doctor looked as if he must have been the oldest doctor in the town.

Joanna showed him her bunions, which had been surgically removed by our very expensive podiatrist in New York, and the doctor wasn't at all fazed by the fact that Joanna had pins in her foot overdue for removal. I watched him walk very slowly over to his antique instruments to choose the ones he would use in the absence of a nurse to hand them to him. A blue liquid was poured over his choice of instruments before he rubbed some alcohol over Joanna's foot and then injected her with a numbing agent that was probably twenty years expired and did absolutely nothing to numb Joanna's foot.

Antonia had stood there motionless from the shock of seeing the Escazu doctor's forceps wiggling and digging inside of her mother's foot, trying to look for the pin with no success. I had tried my best to be strong, until I'd begun to feel I was losing my ability to prevent myself from throwing up and shitting in my pants. I'd had no choice but to leave the operating room.

The Escazu doctor eventually gave up, stitched Joanna's foot up with who-knows-what, and set up a second appointment that would definitely never happen. The "best hospital in Costa Rica" was happy to hand us the bill despite not having done us any favors.

My dermatologist was not from the best hospital. I should have known better, but his service fee fit inside my new budget. The doctor gave me a shot and some cream. It didn't work.

Chapter 54

I WASN'T SURPRISED WHEN THE DARK SIDE OF JACO SAW AN OPENING IN my young wife's spirit; slowly but surely, it worked its way to her control panel. I watched as Cecy began to delve into the passionate beach life as she joined our party-girl waitress Ginger and her newfound Nica friend for multiple shots of tequila more than once a week. Cecy would rarely have a glass of wine once a month before she came to the devil's backyard. My third relationship's snake began to expose its ugly head. I knew if I approached Cecy, she would throw my daily cocktails in my face. The difference between her drinking and mine was that when I was in business, I was able to keep everything in moderation. Cecy wasn't at the point of no control, but I knew what Jaco did for a living, especially to couples. It patiently and precisely burned their initial contracts of love and trust until they had to rewrite them. Phase one of this process had been ignited.

My family was now penniless, and we gradually sold the equipment in Fusion that had any value to the general public in order to survive. I was able to use my old Jaco businessman reputation to negotiate extensions with our utility companies. Cecy and I were running out of options. We together decided that the only place we could work to eat was at my ex-wife's eclectic restaurant at her home. I called her to find out that she was more than happy to accommodate us. Joanna knew we were professional servers, and like many people who laid eyes on our child, she adored Lucy.

Joanna's restaurant had consistent customers. Most of her customers were part of our expatriate world who had frequented Valle Azul when we owned it, and the other fairly large share of attendees were tourists who'd been referred by high-end bed-and-breakfast hotels or had seen a positive write-up about Joanna's restaurant in a magazine. Joanna had a unique menu that blended a variety of delicious flavors with extremely healthy foods. I could not be more impressed with my ex-wife; she hadn't been able to cook a hot dog when I'd first met her.

Cecy and I went right to work at Joanna's restaurant; we were both professionals and knew how to handle everything down to decanting a bottle of red wine. I realized how happy I was taking care of customers in a functioning restaurant. I would sometimes glance over to Cecy to observe her glamorous looks and smile stimulating each table. I thought I had made the right decision to join with Joanna to give first-class service to first-class food.

The ex-wife-and-wife waltz was fine for the first week; everybody was able to dodge the ego game, at least according to my perception! My IQ was definitely not as high as I had thought it was. The first question on an IQ test should be: *Do you think that everything is going to be okay if you take your beautiful and young new wife to the vice president of the Bitter Middle-Aged Women's Club's home, everybody would be one big, happy family?* The examiner would have sent me directly to the monkey farm after the first answer.

There are times in life that remind us that civilization was not built by civilized people; it was built through wars. I was hustling my ass off, taking care of the tables—we had to serve and bus the tables—and I was taking a break to sip a glass of wine when the ex-wife's friend jokingly pointed to all the dishes in the sink and said, "The sink is full. Now you have to wash dishes." Joanna always had a dishwasher; I guess she hadn't shown up that day.

I would of course have been willing to help out by washing the dishes until I heard Joanna's *other* voice say, "Wash the dishes, bitch." It was the witching hour I always tried to avoid like the plague; Joanna had drunk the final cocktail required to allow Katherine to take control. At this point in my life, for the most part, I didn't care how low I'd have to go to survive, but no one would call me a bitch. I stood in place and remained silent as Katherine tried to take her control over me and my family to another level. She said something to Cecy I didn't hear, but I knew Cecy well enough to see in her eyes that my present wife wanted someone dead.

I had been married to Joanna for twenty-two years. I knew her life, and I knew the majority of her dreams were nightmares. When Katherine visited, she wanted to reenact Joanna's dreams in real life. If one allowed the dreams to come to life, they'd better be ready to welcome Armageddon.

I could see that Cecy wanted me to protect her from Katherine's words. I knew for the sake of all parties involved that it would be better for her and me to take what we came with and leave.

The bottom was dropping out from under our feet. When we returned to Jaco, the decision was made for Cecy to take Lucy and return to her mother's home in Panama. Fusion was almost depleted of products and would not support the survival of three people. We sold the air conditioners in Fusion to give Cecy a little bit of survival pocket money and to buy enough gas for me to drive Cecy and Lucy to Panama before returning to Jaco to continue my war for survival there and try to secure an income.

As we drove to Panama, I knew my wife was very angry. I thought, *She loves me, and she has walked through hell with me, so someday I will change our nightmare into a sweet dream.*

Chapter 55

When I returned from Panama, I entered Fusion with no game plan whatsoever. How would one make a plan under these circumstances? Every party who was involved in the mortgage scam was most likely praying every day that I would never get the funds to build a legal support system that was capable of easily proving their breach of contract. I consistently tortured my mind with images of the same situation happening in the United States; the property would have automatically been returned to me along with select parties at Daystar being fired or even arrested. I wasn't in the United States; I was under a legal system of bright people who made it impossible to see through the fog of unlimited corruption in their country.

I decided to take another trip to Panama to visit my family after only a few weeks. I let a basic nomad gringo from Philadelphia named Kyle have a roommate space in the restaurant while I was away. I knew he was a criminal runaway, but he had a decent heart. Foolishly, I once again put a person in my trust zone to avoid being lonely.

I didn't care about myself when I returned to Jaco; my family's security, especially when it came to my children losing their inheritance, was my number one concern. I was broke. The only option I had left was to mix my past reputation with sensitivity to try to steer the Daystar partners into doing the right thing. I was grateful that my twenty-five-year-old Kia Sportage had been able to struggle through another trip from Panama to Costa Rica. Fusion seemed secured from break-ins. I wanted to rest and design another plan to avoid losing absolutely everything I had left.

I had a decent offer for a kind of famous abstract painting of a fisherman's fantasy painting that was hanging on the wall. I decided to sell it for fast food and gas money. When I walked to the wall to observe the picture one last time, it was gone. My mind immediately flashed back to a Facebook photo of Kyle and his broken group of derelict gringos having a great time on the beach. It wasn't hard to figure out that my fantasy fish painting had financed their party.

It would have been better to leave a scarecrow in blackface to guard my property during my second trip to visit my family. I should have known

Kyle was going to sell the picture after his girlfriend had indirectly offered to trade sex for it before I had left. She was actually quite beautiful, yet the problem was I had spent too many hours listening to Kyle's indications that he might carry a special disease. It was difficult enough to stay faithful to my wife, but any of the many women Kyle pointed a finger at was definitely not an option. I tried very hard to give Kyle a nice-sounding reason to look for another place to stay.

Chapter 56

THE TELEVISIONS, FOOD, AND LIQUOR WERE GONE; THOSE ITEMS HAD been our lifeblood when my family was with me. All I had left to sell to survive was the very expensive sound system.

I decided to no longer give free rides with my Kia. I had been giving free rides to people I knew, mainly Mark Art, but now if anyone wanted a ride down the street, they had to pay. I called Allen, a fellow expatriate and alumni of my high school, who ran a hotel in Manuel Antonio, and I made a deal with him to bring tourists into his business for commission. My ex-roommate Kyle worked at a fishing yacht company and was more than happy to pay me commissions for fishing trip referrals.

I would sit down at popular bars and restaurants and start having a beer or two—or three, four, or five—to meet tourists who had questions about what to do next in Costa Rica. I was a people person, a professional sales executive. My small business plan slowly but surely started to fall into place. My twenty-year-old Kia Sportage became "Tony's Tours." I was making enough survival money to guarantee at least one *casado* (cheap typical meal) per day. I decided to visit my family in Panama again after I secured a multiple-day tourist run that lasted long enough to fund my trip. I missed my family; I needed security hugs as I reassured them I was going to make everything OK and made a small financial contribution to their well-being.

Chapter 57

THE TRIP FROM JACO TO PANAMA WAS EXTRAORDINARILY BEAUTIFUL. The landscape, decorated with the finest fauna and flora, presented a visual concerto of the reasons Central American life fascinated the people of the world. I never regretted the opportunity to view Mother Nature's blessings of Costa Rica and Panama. The first six hours of my drive was a spiritual gourmet. I had thus far driven in forty-five states and thirty-five countries, and the drive from Costa Rica to Panama was among my top three favorites.

Robles was a very unique town; somehow, it would always find another reason to celebrate life. I arrived just in time to dance the last salsas and merengues with Cecy. I could not help but notice how my wife's beauty and charisma stood steps above the crowd; she once again proudly presented her gringo husband to her neighbors who were consistently hoping she would join their group of abandonment. I hated every day I was without my family; I knew every day we spent apart was a gamble on my part to lose the family I loved with all of my heart. Of course, I felt a little awkward knowing Cecy was twenty-five years younger than me, yet I kept explaining why the backbone of social connotations didn't apply to our special relationship.

Cecy showed me her love for me that night, but I felt I had lost a small part of her. Inside my mind, I felt I was becoming more of a figurehead than a husband and father. I knew my wife didn't like questions that had the potential to lead to a negative subject, so I took the path of nonresistance to once again keep the peace in our relationship of tolerance.

As symbolic as it may seem, my last legitimate income-producer and mode of connection with my family died while I was in Panama. My very old but faithful Kia's motor breathed its last breath.

I'd thought I was on a stable path to spirituality before I'd moved to Costa Rica. I had engulfed myself in reading the Old Testament, the Torah, the Tibetan Book of Living and Dying, the Egyptian Book of the Dead, and the translations of Sumer's *Earth Chronicles*. I tried to be a better person even though I continued to make bad decisions. I had been honest and fair with my employees who were accustomed to being abused by a very high percentage of their Central and South American employers.

I couldn't help but think I had been missing something extremely huge in the way I was conducting my life. Maybe things like voodoo and witchcraft actually existed, and maybe I was the ignorant so-called intellectual gringo who simply did not understand the reality of the true culture of Central America. I kept getting my ass handed to me without understanding why I kept falling into every crack that opened. If I had the answer, I was too afraid and embarrassed to acknowledge it.

Chapter 58

I KNEW I WAS GAMBLING WITH MY LIFE AND MY MARRIAGE WHEN I boarded the bus back to Costa Rica. I had to figure out a way to make a deal to offset the mortgage or sell Fusion. Fusion was the only thing I had left to create a base to give my family a new start in the United States. I knew my Central American days were over after losing my life of luxury. I was desperately trying to not return to the States with absolutely nothing.

I decided to get in touch with every Realtor I knew and every contact I had to try to find the golden needle in the haystack. I could not understand why I was only receiving questions, but no offers, about a property located in one of the most exposed locations in Jaco. I found myself at times trying not to think that I or the property had been cursed. I took into account the bloodstain on the floor that had been left by the murderer's standoff with the police, and I lowered the price accordingly. All of the potential buyers were either superstitious or a lot shrewder than me.

I had put the family I loved with all of my heart on the sacrificial slab. I was determined to win; I hated losing. My mind covered my eyes as it drank a cocktail of stubbornness and selfishness. They were love's greatest competitors.

Even though my guardian angels continued to enforce their eye-opening punishment of my choices, they would once in a while throw me a "mommy bone." Mothers, no matter how angry or disgusted they are with their children, will always remind them that they are one of the unconditional loves of their lives.

A young Tico man walked directly toward me one day as I was sitting on my restaurant patio, once again waiting for a semi-miracle. I had been in Costa Rica long enough to know that if someone had focused their radar on me, this Tico was on a mission, because there wasn't much left in the restaurant. After selling everything that was mobile to survive for the past three months, I just hoped this man was the angel who had the magical solution to solve my expanding nightmare. He walked into Fusion like he was a detective at a crime scene.

"How can I help you?" I decided to break the ice and start the conversation.

"¿Cómo estás, Tony? Pura Vida!" the young Tico said confidently. He knew exactly who I was. Ticos prided themselves on doing enough homework to know who's who.

"*Eso es,*" I replied, a typical response in Costa Rica to the greeting *Pura Vida*. "Muy bien, gracias," I continued, "*¿Cómo se llama y cómo puedo ayudar?*" (What is your name and how can I help you?).

"*Mi nombre es DJ,*" he replied. "*Quiero comprar su equipo DJ.*" (My name is DJ. I want to buy your DJ equipment). All I wanted to do was to survive. DJ had my full attention.

I was quite impressed with my visitor's business demeanor. DJ inspected the lighting and sound equipment thoroughly. It was the only equipment I had left, and I never thought anyone in Jaco would have the interest, income, or external funds to purchase the equipment. I had been using the equipment to urge potential buyers of the property to take a more serious consideration toward buying.

Having heard my awkward Spanish, DJ switched to English. "I'm a DJ, you have good equipment, and I need some speakers. How much?"

The speakers retailed at $250 each. My stomach took over my mind. I didn't want to lose this DJ, especially if he had the money to feed this now unemployed squatter.

"*Sesenta cinco mil colones cada una,*" (Sixty-five thousand colones—$150—for each one) I replied. I blurted this out after pretending to actually think about it. I was desperate, and everybody within a hundred-mile radius knew it. It seemed like I'd metamorphosed from one of the most successful businessmen in Costa Rica to a pauper overnight. I tried to go over in my head how I could so gradually fuck up my life, but my mind was in survival mode; it had no time or space to process my self-pity.

"*Cincuenta mil colones cada una; necesito dos para ahora*" ($100 each; I need two for now).

I could tell DJ was a seasoned Tico businessman. I had dealt with many entrepreneurs on this continent at this point, including my former father-in-law, yet a real Tico businessman surpassed most when it came to negotiating a deal.

I knew to never take the first offer in Costa Rica even if I was obviously drooling at the mouth. "*Ciento veinticinco,*" ($125) I said after once again pretending to think hard about his offer. I used my IBM training and waited for DJ to reply. I was out of resources; I no longer had a car with which to create survival income.

DJ agreed to my "fire sale" offer for the speakers. *"Esta bien!"* (OK!)

I didn't understand how to measure how stubborn I was being; I had been squatting on my property for four months while trying to sell it at what I considered to be a 75 percent discount. DJ had slowly but surely acquired the complete sound system a month later. With every day that passed, the odds of me eating the next day continued to decrease.

My circle of derelict friends became much more valuable to me. Mark Art was such a talented artist, and he would continue to be hired by local businesses to do murals. Mark Art's problem was that he was a helpless romantic and loved to party; his money would flow like an open faucet. My problem, of course, was that my finances were always nil to none; every day, when I woke up, I would try to prepare myself to not think about food. When Mark Art hit bottom, he would easily find me sitting on the patio of my restaurant. We'd find out how many coins I had to join him to buy some cheap pasta, canned sauce, and a cheap bottle of wine.

Mark Art was not the only Mark in my circle. When I'd first met the other Mark, he'd reminded me of Pat Boone, the epitome of handsome and suave. I'd thought he was easily a multimillionaire; how wrong was I! The advantage Mark had over me was that he was living in a friend's apartment with luxuries such as hot water, a real bed, a refrigerator, and a television.

Mark and I made a bond of survival; he became my brother and my confidant. Mark and I would sit on my restaurant's patio every day and wait for one of our friends or relatives to send us a text or email with a Western Union number. The financial gifts would become rarer as time passed, but when one of us got one, we would drink and feast together.

The power of deprivation was especially amazing to me; I'd hardly known the word existed in what seemed to now be my past life. How arrogant I had been in taking absolutely everything for granted! The materials of life had been practically falling into my lap; I'd never once stopped to think how blessed I'd been to have a bed, clean water, and food. In New York, after Joanna and I would enjoy one of her delicious gourmet dinners, she would hand me the *Gourmet* magazine and have me choose another "cuisine challenge" for her to make the next day. We had never once worried about the cost of the prime meats needed to prepare our meals!

Chapter 59

THE SIXTH MONTH OF MY PERSONAL NIGHTMARE BLANKETED MY LIFE in a deep depression. My health was a daily roll of the dice. I always woke up hungry and lonely, and I just hated the days when my feet would swell badly and give me such intense pain that I had to hobble to the bathroom using one of the last two bar stools just to get there before I pissed on myself.

I was sitting on the patio, keeping myself sane one day, not minding my business at all, when in the distance, I observed a woman, a young man, and a little boy walking down the main street toward Fusion. I thought, *This is nothing out of the ordinary. Many people pass Fusion to visit the many families in the "worker-bee" neighborhood down the street from the building or to go to the beach.*

As the family came closer to Fusion, it became extremely difficult not to focus on the woman. She was reasonably pretty, but she didn't need to be any more than that; her body more than completed the formula for me to consider her completely desirable.

As the family gradually advanced closer to my patio, I realized that I was their bull's-eye, especially as the very familiar "Jaco Beach negotiation" smiles exploded on their faces.

"Hello, how are you?" the woman greeted me in English.

I had been in Jaco long enough to usually know what I was dealing with in these cases, although I had been surprised one or two times. "I'm good! *¿Cómo están?*" (How are all of you?) I returned with a mix of English and Spanish to give them a signal that I could work with them in both languages if needed. It had been a long time since I'd been with my wife, so I was more than pleased to have the company of such a pretty lady.

"My name is Joanne," she said. "This is my brother Richard and my son Byron. We're from Venezuela."

They were very polite; I saw no threat whatsoever. "*Con mucho gusto; bienvenido,*" (Very nice to meet you; welcome) I said. I knew one thing about how to navigate Jaco: if you are not sure, get to the point. "*¿Cómo puedo ayudarte?*" (How can I help you?) This sexually deprived man had to try extremely hard to keep his eyes in the right place. My mother had tried very hard to make me and my brothers gentlemen. Some of us slipped through the cracks; I was her best student though I occasionally tilted.

"Byron has a school project, and he needs supplies," she said. "I can't afford them, and I was wondering if he could use some things in your restaurant to complete his project?"

Joanne hit all of my sensitivities when it came to children and education. I immediately opened my entire restaurant to Byron. I'll never forget his smile when he found everything he needed. I even gave them my valuable leftover pizza from Mike's restaurant.

Joanne and her family hugged me before leaving.

Chapter 60

I BECAME MORE SENSITIVE TO THE "GRINGO GHOST" AS I WOULD LIMP the quarter mile to the drug store. I never officially met or spent time with the Gringo Ghost; he'd knocked on my back door one morning when my family was still with me, desperate for any kind of alcohol. I gave him a small bottle and told him not to return; off he went to be very happy.

When I sat on my patio, I would watch the Gringo Ghost practically dance to the beach to see his daughter. As time went by, he evolved from a typical stumbling alcoholic to a suave Cary Grant on excellent drugs. I had a mixed bag of feelings for the Gringo Ghost; I admired the fact that he was happy with his mix of alcohol and drugs, but I also knew that his ex-wife hated him—and his daughter barely tolerated their deteriorating icon of freedom.

Chapter 61

DURING THE SIXTH MONTH OF LIVING IN THE ABANDONED FUSION building, my health started to quickly deteriorate. My skin was getting harder and turning blacker than I was. There were even some days I couldn't walk because my foot and ankle swelled up to twice their normal size, creating enough pain to push anyone to the edge of insanity. I borrowed money in the streets to buy eight hundred-milligram ibuprofen capsules, and I would take two capsules every eight hours until I could walk again.

A dull flicker of light in my life was my gradual adoption into my new Venezuelan friend's family. Joanne and her family returned on a day during which I'd already determined I would not have the means to eat. They brought me some buttered pasta that they'd managed to squeeze out of their own food provisions.

It was difficult resisting the temptation as Joanne used her perfect hourglass body to practice her client-seduction routines on me. I was a starving and insecure man who needed all of the ego I could scrape off the vaulted ceiling.

Joanne, even though her name was too close for comfort to my ex-wife's, made me feel special; she reminded me that I still had some kick in my step.

Joanne and her family started to become part of my survival circle. They became a very important part of my Jaco life, and I didn't want to do anything to lose them.

Chapter 62

"Mommy *está pasando*" were the words that innocently came out of my daughter Lucy's mouth over the phone the night I called to check in with my family.

My heart filled with pain; my spirit began to crumble as I asked my baby girl to repeat what she'd said. "*¿Que?*" I asked, hoping for new words.

"Mommy está pasando *esta noche.*"

I hadn't seen my family for five months. I knew I should have walked away from my attempts to sell Fusion and figured out a way to return to North America with my small emergency fund and restart my family's life, but I still had legal rights to sell the property and save a skeleton of financial security. I didn't or couldn't accept the fact that Jaco was now a penny-on-the-dollar buyers' market. The market that had created the $800,000 offer had sailed five years ago.

"Pasando" in Spanish many times means going on a date with someone or other intimate activities. I wasn't sure what was going on, but I knew I had a wife who most men would die for just from initial observation. I had been covering my ailments, insecurities, and sadness in front of my acquaintances and the many strangers who walked by my defunct business. Losing my family was a tipping point.

I had been able to create a mental security night routine for the past six months: waiting for the mosquitos to finish their meal, laying down on my hard mat to have a conversation with myself, and finally praying to my guardians to protect me from the people in Costa Rica who wanted to hurt me.

I was trying to win a hopeless war of principles using integrity and charm; it was all I had left. The thousand-square-meter property situated one hundred meters from the beach was not even selling for the price of the mortgage. Not only did I not know whether I'd be able to eat every day; I now had sickening visions in my head of my wife starting to date other men!

A dark mental slime slowly covered my mind. This was the beginning of a final conversation inside myself. *Why am I holding on to my property like a baby with its comfort blanket?* I saw an image in my mind of my two-story,

2,500 square foot Panama City ocean-view penthouse apartment, filled with the finest furniture. I remembered how I'd felt in my new $40,000 SUV emulating a jaguar, transgressing the Central American countryside. I remembered how I'd smiled at the first-class attention given to my family by the waiters at choice restaurants whenever we walked in to enjoy a meal, every meal perfectly cooked to each person's specifications. I remembered how I'd arrogantly sipped my Chivas whiskey and sampled fine wine to mingle with my fine dinners.

As I contemplated my past and lost life, the darkness slowly surrounded me with joy as I listened to every inviting word that resounded in my mind. *How could I be so careless? What was I thinking? I didn't do my homework.* Once again, I'd thought my life—even after I'd lost the Torreys and the 1 percent family I'd married into as go-to options—would fix itself.

My routine changed after I'd heard my daughter's innocent words; I had been designing an "if all else fails" plan. I knew exactly where little strange round white pills for or against your health existed throughout the restaurant. I didn't know exactly what they were used for, but I thought maybe there were enough to solve my problem.

I was betraying my mind, soul, and spirit. My guardians were very sad and disappointed with their vehicle whom they had trusted to protect myself and them from obscurity's destructive forces. I was tired; I began to forget I was one of the many children of the "Great Light and Love." I just wanted to avoid the next dawn.

Chapter 63

To my surprise, I woke up the following day. I got up and tried walking to the bathroom, but my mind and body were completely off-balance. I paused, waiting to see if this problem was going to be permanent, before continuing the treacherous journey to the bathroom.

I washed what I could of my body with the iguana water I collected from the roof of the restaurant, brushed my teeth, and walked out to the patio to take up my position of waiting for something good to fall from the sky or a Western Union text to appear on my phone.

I had never realized how much my mind was married to suffering. I didn't remember seeing or hearing birds until the morning I should not have seen. Hundreds of beautiful multicolored macaws emerged from the trees across from the restaurant, their tenor voices rejoicing as they flew toward the beach. Then, hundreds of beautiful parakeets, all different shades of green, followed them from the same groups of trees, merging their soprano voices with the macaws' tenors.

My beautiful neighbors seemed to have increased their volume to introduce my awareness back into the beauty of our earth and the gift of life the Creator assigned us to protect. When my beautiful macaws and parakeets flew in unison to their respective branches at dusk, I realized that someone who loved me was opening my eyes to life's value. I knew I had to work through my problems and return to my family. A powerful energy surrounded me, and I knew I wanted to live—no matter what it took.

Chapter 64

My Venezuelan family would consistently visit to share whatever resources we could dig up together. I was very happy whenever my substitute family came by. Joanne was an eyeful, especially when she would sport her bikinis. The boys treated me like I was her husband.

I liked the nonphysical status of our connection; it actually seemed to make our bond stronger. I was actually impressed with how I could be with a sex goddess and not follow through with sex.

Joanne, on the other hand, had other plans; I think the fact that her family loved me and that I was hands-off with her put me on a special level with her, much higher than any of her other clients.

In the middle of one of my substitute family's many deprivation get-togethers, Joanne pulled me inside of Fusion, put her body up against mine, looked me in the eyes, and said, "Tony, we want you to live with us. If you do, I will make love to you every night."

My "X chromosome" ego immediately jumped in and stopped my thought process completely; he wanted me to understand exactly what was happening. This was an automatic yes for him. My "Y chromosome" ego pushed its way into my mind and started rattling off my real family's names—*Cecy, Lucy, Nico, Antonia*—and reminded me that I would be second, third, or fourth wheel every single one of those love-making nights with Joanne since she was a sex worker. I really wanted to listen to "X;" he made a lot of sense when he said, "Ask yourself how many opportunities like this is a fifty-five-year-old man going to get." Even though X's proposal was extremely tempting, my "Y" had a much stronger argument than my "X." I politely refused Joanne's offer and listened to "X" crying like a baby in my head.

A tennis partner of mine, Mike, had a popular restaurant in Jaco. He saw my life joining the many of those who'd made the same decisions of demise. Mike offered me a free pizza at any time I needed to eat; it was embarrassing, but I had to accept his generosity when I was very hungry. I had to walk over my ego to survive. I would literally drag myself to his restaurant, but when I got there, the staff always showed me the utmost respect. They gave me love one specific day when I defied their conceptions of "normal" gringo behavior in Latin America by crying over the loss of my third world Panamanian wife's *abuelo* (grandfather). I knew I had admired Abuelo, but I had no idea I had loved him until I found myself unable to stop the tears in the middle of the restaurant after I heard he had passed.

Abuelo had been the epitome of a Panamanian patriarch; he was well into his eighties when I'd met him. Abuelo and Abuela (Grandmother) had been very skeptical when they first met me; as a matter of fact, they wouldn't have given me the time of day. They had seen over and over again how arrogant older gringos would court their beautiful young daughters, get them pregnant, and disappear into the night. I'd understood how they felt; I had lived in Central America for ten years by the time I'd met them and had also observed the abusive mixed-culture relationships. In my heart, I knew my relationship with Cecy was different; I felt true love for Cecy. Of course, the age difference made me and anyone else involved a little uncomfortable, but I truly loved Cecy and had been willing to solve any labyrinth to help open their hearts so they would be able to feel mine.

Abuelo would limp to his hammock every day to spend a short time with his family. Abuelo's house sat at the intersection of two streets and was five hundred yards from the entrance of the Panamanian Highway. One of the streets was heavily occupied by one of their daughter's children and grandchildren, and the other street sheltered their other daughters and their grandchildren. Abuelo's only son, Chico, ran his soldering business out of the house in order to be close to his parents. I had watched in envy how my wife's family merged together and took care of each other. I had wanted Cecy, but I'd also wanted to be part of such a beautiful family. I had asked her parents' permission to marry her, and I knew I had the approval of Abuelo when he'd looked at me with love in his eyes as he handed me Cecy's hand in marriage. I was family and had Abuelo's official blessing to sit at his home, located in the center of their family's homes, and respond to the many *saludas* (greetings) that rode the breezes to the home.

I always loved my visits with Cecy's family for the first three days; any longer, and I would start reaching deep into my patience bag to tolerate the amazingly high level of gossip that would take place with the women in her family. It never stopped; whether they were cooking or playing bingo, or the Mariachis were playing live, they continued to gossip. There were no sports on TV; the TVs were playing shows that had aired when I had been growing up and had a black-and-white television. If it wasn't for Cecy's father being my drinking buddy, I would have just wanted to lay down and die after the third day of visiting.

Robles, the "Peyton Place soap opera" of Panama, did like to party; any excuse that town could create to party, they would use, bringing music to the town recreation area and dancing the night away. I always hoped they had scheduled a party every time I came to visit; I would be dancing at least one night each visit.

I greatly missed my life in Panama, and not being there at the time that Abuelo passed away was yet another image of my life falling apart.

I had a little pride left, and I did not want to beg. My only alternative to begging was to return to my ex-wife's illegal restaurant to be a waiter. My oldest daughter, Antonia, from time to time would send me a little survival cash. I once used some of the funds to have a great lunch out with my son, Nico. After our lunch, I rushed to catch the bus to get to my shift at Joanna's restaurant. I was not proud to have to be subservient to Joanna, but I was out of resources—and it was one of the last two places I could find a meal. A policeman was waiting in front of the bus door when I arrived. He had some papers and pointed to where I should sign them. I thought it had to do with my property; I thought the papers he was giving me to sign were standard practice for the process of retaining my property. I wasn't thinking at all, and I didn't read the papers; I was still euphoric after having such a great lunch with my son. I signed them and boarded the bus to Escazu to work for food at Joanna's.

My alter ego was still from the ghetto; he was storing many years of the anger I'd had to ignore in order to be able to endure my evolution of lives from the ghetto to Costa Rica. "Alter" was disappointed in me; he wanted to release the anger, the violence, and the fight I'd been born with and explode, tearing Joanna's house down. My delicately developed intellectual side was strong enough to contain "Alter," but it was degrading each day. I could hear "Alter" every night screaming at me: *Tony! How do you feel being your ex-wife's slave? How do you really fucking feel?* "Alter" was humiliated; he wanted me to release him. I needed "Alter" more than I had thought I did; my present actions of survival were shaming us to a point of no return. I knew if I acted on his ghetto thoughts, I could lose everything I had, including all my children.

I didn't want to feel. I knew the exact feeling that was waiting to enter me. I had to keep humiliation out. It teased me, confident in the fact that it would sooner or later get in. Joanna's 11:00 a.m. happy hours helped coat my self-esteem enough to pretend I was not noticing the debilitating situation in which I resided. I would try to make myself feel better by reminding myself that the woman who had me encased as a fifth-class citizen used to tell me I was "the love of her life." I loved the side of Joanna that children saw—her intrigue and her free spirit—but I hated Katherine. Katherine had used to tolerate me, but she, like Joanna's father, was tired of us fucking up our lives, walking ass-backwards. I consistently designed mental formulas to block the feelings that would interfere with what little I had left in my life. There was no other choice than to accept my new position, at least until it became unbearable.

Katherine showed up like it was her last dance one night in front of the entire staff a few weeks after I'd returned to her restaurant for work. I knew it hadn't been Joanna; Joanna went to sleep whenever Katherine would take over. I could easily be located on the first bus back to Jaco the following morning.

Being a restaurant caveman with a leveled bed and iguana feces water didn't seem so bad when I returned home from Joanna's. The local assholes had ripped me off, taking everything they'd felt had some value, including the cereal Nuria's mother had given me out of pity after she saw how much weight I had lost. I stopped caring. I had never felt more alone in all my years that I had been so far allotted by my Creator.

Mark was happy to have his patio partner back. The daytime temperatures in Jaco ranged from ninety-one to one hundred degrees. Mark and I would gather whatever spare change or borrowing power we had to eat a cheap meal and hopefully have enough left over to enjoy a beer or two as we watched the people and traffic buzz through the main entrance into Jaco Beach. I entertained myself many times by watching the local buses show off their U-turn skills without hitting one of the electric poles at the corner of Fusion.

Chapter 65

WHY SO MANY JACO POLICE CARS? I THOUGHT. THEY WERE COMING directly toward Fusion. The next thought that entered my mind was: *What the hell did Mark do?* I had met many gringos who were sooner or later picked up by the Costa Rican police or the International Police, so I wasn't too surprised that it was happening again, but I didn't want to lose the one person who had almost struggled with me as much as I had. Mark was like the only family I had left.

The police cars stopped, surrounding Fusion at the left, center, and right of the entrance. I felt I had jumped into the middle of a full-blown action movie. Six policemen jumped quickly out of the cars and surrounded me. "*Manos atrás*," (hands behind) one policeman said to me, not Mark.

I put my hands behind my back for the first time in my life and asked, "*¿Qué pasó?*" (What happened?) They were silent as they put me in a car and drove me to jail.

The police informed me that I had twenty-four hours to pay four hundred dollars to be released from the local jail, and if I didn't pay the four hundred dollars, I would be sent to the long-term prison for six months.

Most Ticos thought that four hundred dollars was just a phone call away for expats. Maybe for a lot of other people it was—for me, it would have been in what was now my past life—but I hadn't seen more than forty dollars at one time in my present life. There were no "help wanted" signs for high-paying jobs in my cell. I had used up all of my favors with anyone who cared about me, and the police were not giving me my one phone call anyway.

I spent the entire sleepless night evaluating each action that had sent me down my life's steps of complete failure. I frustrated myself by trying to lay the blame, but eventually and angrily, I accepted the fact that I had lost complete focus and left a huge door open for any semi-clever entity to take whatever they wanted.

My death certificate was waiting for its final signature. I was twice as old as 90 percent of the most dangerous prisoners in Central and South America who occupied the prison I would be sent to the following morning. If I was the person I had been six months ago, I would have had a fighting chance, but now I was unhealthy and penniless. I didn't even smoke what ex-convicts called lifesaving cigarettes. I gave myself thirty to sixty days before someone at that prison would relieve me of my misery.

Twenty-three of my twenty-four hours were up. The policeman now felt bad for this gringo who had done nothing but positive things for Jaco. He opened my cell and led me to a desk; he needed to complete the paperwork required to secure me a six-month sentence in one of the most dangerous prisons in Central America. My trip to the prison would more than tag this sick, hungry, and penniless gringo as a "dead man walking," and he knew it. Maybe I should have been a little more sensitive when I'd told an already-scorned Nuria that I felt she had only wanted to marry me for my money at a time when her scorned mother pitied me enough to donate groceries to who should have been her son-in-law.

I had nothing more to say or think; I just watched as the officer signed my life away and restricted my passport so I could not leave Costa Rica. He pushed the papers across the table to me, and I signed them without asking a question or giving my best performance of self-destruction a single thought. I started accepting my demise. I had lost!

I didn't see Mike come into the police station while I was signing the papers. Mike, the restaurant owner that would give me free pizza, stood beside me and spoke perfect Spanish to the officer. The officer pointed Mike to another desk, turned to me, and gave me a huge smile of relief. I didn't know exactly what was happening until Mike returned to where I was sitting and said with his strong Austrian Arnold Schwarzenegger accent, "Tony, you're free." Mike put his hand on my shoulder and said, "Let's get out of here."

How could I thank this man who had actually saved my life? All I could do was hug him. Mike had been in Jaco for thirty years, and the streets of Jaco and Costa Rica had ears that could hear what was happening, especially information about a gringo as well-known as I. Mike knew as soon as he'd heard what was happening to me that within thirty days, he would have lost one of his sunset beer and tennis partners forever. Not all angels are in spiritual form.

"Tony, you need to make a decision," Mike said. He wanted to make sure I understood exactly what he was saying. He looked me directly in the eyes until I responded.

"I understand," I replied.

We set up a meeting at his restaurant the following day.

I knew that I had to act on Mike's words. It was time to cut the Costa Rica cord and accept that my life was more important than my livelihood. I was extremely angry at the mother of my son. Faith in her rationality was no longer an option. I had lived long enough as a gringo male in Central America to know the truth: there were so many low-life trailer trash gringo men who used and abused beautiful young Latinas who were donated by their families to these rejects from the United States in hopes that it would help their daughters eat or upgrade their lives. The end results usually created a lost child with blue eyes.

Nuria was different; she was a small businesswoman, as smart as any lawyer who could create programs to make sure gringos contributed to their child's health and welfare. I respected that part of her, but she'd underestimated my love and commitment to my son. I don't think she understood that my finances were depleted when she threw me into the ring of life and death for failing to support him.

Chapter 66

I WAITED FOR MIKE TO DO HIS ROUTINE RITUAL OF COURTING HIS customers at each table. Mike's staff continued to push whatever I wanted to eat or drink in my direction. Most Ticos who worked in the tourist industry emulated the selfishness of the industry's culture. Mike's employees were very different; each one of them was a long-term employee who'd basically started with Mike right after dropping out of or finishing high school. Mike's family of service workers were one of the most well-known families in Jaco.

Mike walked over to me wearing the same look he would have when explaining to me how we needed to adjust our game plan as a double's tennis team. Mike's game was at least two grades higher than mine, so I had no choice but to listen and try to obey his instructions. I would always get a tickle listening to Mike's Arnold Schwarzenegger accent.

Mike stood at the small high table I was sitting at in the restaurant's bar area, looked me directly in the eyes, laid an envelope on the table, and got straight to the reason he was meeting with me: "There are fifteen hundred dollars in the envelope; it's the standard price to bribe your way out of the country." Before I started to cry or hug him, he said, "My employees made some phone calls to their friends and families to find out the best person who can help you. The guy was a politician in Puerto Viejo, where you will need to cross over to Panama." Mike handed me a small, neatly folded piece of paper. "Contact him when you get there." Mike looked me even deeper into my eyes. "Tony! Don't trust anyone; they will kill you for this much money."

I took the money and the paper; my terror had displaced my urge to cry. I had seen way too many documentaries about people trying to escape third world countries and ending up with a judge giving them even longer sentences than they would've had on shit's row in some of the worst prisons in each of the respective countries. I had to come to the realization that this middle-aged, undernourished, and displaced cultural conversion kit was about to once again put his life on the line to climb out of his Central American nightmare. I gave Mike a big hug, waved to the staff, took the rest of the free pizza, and limped back to my purgatory, where I continued to contemplate what the hell had happened to my life.

Chapter 67

I WOKE THE NEXT MORNING KIND OF HOPING THAT WHAT HAD HAPPENED the day before was a dream. I knew I had to try to escape; I had no choice. Mike had made it clear that his help was a one-time and final offer. After my bout with the dark spirits a few weeks before, I'd woken up knowing I wanted to live—if not for me, for my children. The issue that confused me at this point was how I would get back to the States if I made it to Panama. I knew I'd have to beg for at least five hundred dollars more to buy a one-way ticket.

Phone cards had become my best friend; I used various ways to contact family members to ask them to send me whatever they could spare. My base family members had run out of spares, especially my mother, who was so generous that she'd depleted her entire savings account trying to save this sinking ghost ship. I knew some people I had supported financially who'd never needed to return the favor in the past. This was the moment of truth for me that people all over the world have witnessed or lived: the time when one finds out who their true friends are.

I had to limp back to the Mas Por Menos grocery store at least five times over the following few days to buy phone cards before I finally dialed one of my cousins who had visited me once in Costa Rica. She was more than happy to help me save my life.

The other donor was my little buddy Brad whose parents were two of my best friends. Brad and his two friends had come to visit me in Jaco during their college spring break and had crashed my GM truck. It had cost many thousands of dollars for me to fix, so I put him on my list. Brad was shocked as all hell to hear from me, but he was even more surprised when he was told why. After a formal greeting, I got serious with him: "Remember the accident you and your friends had with my truck?"

"Yes," Brad said, waiting to hear the rest of my statement.

"Do you remember when I said that one day in the future, I might call in my chip?"

"Yes!" he replied.

"Brad, I would never contact you if it wasn't very important; I need to call in that chip."

Brad was from the 10 percent, and I knew he would be extremely surprised by a phone call from someone who had been part of the 1 percent. Brad had a decent job, but he was by no means well-off; I loved him like he was my own son, and he was one of the last people I wanted to call.

"Tony, I'm moving to California and my fiancée is moving in with me; I'm very short on cash," he replied.

I hesitated, letting my shame paint my insides; I was practically this young man's second father. I had to swallow the little pride I had left. "Brad, I would have never asked you to pay anything. I know it was an accident. I'm stuck in Costa Rica, and I need money to get the hell out of here. I'm running out of people who will help me. What can you do?"

Brad hesitated for a few seconds. "Tony, I can send you five hundred dollars. Will that help?"

I was happy about the contributions I'd gotten, but at the same time, I was extremely disappointed in my pretend friends who actually owed me money and were scattering like roaches in a bathroom when the lights turn on. Brad's words put me in the final position to give myself a chance to save my life and get back to the home where I could be free.

Chapter 68

I BOUGHT A LARGE BOTTLE OF CHEAP VODKA AND GOT DRUNK WITH MY group of derelicts for the last time. I was actually going to miss this special survival circle we had formed; it was of an awkward brotherhood, but it functioned.

I had matured and been abused enough in my Central American life to know not to say a word or let anyone buy a vowel about what I was about to embark on. It was extremely difficult not to say anything about my upcoming attempt to escape the country, especially when I spoke to Mark, my patio brother.

When a Tico says that word of mouth is the best advertising one can do in Costa Rica, they are not kidding. By the time my last business had closed in Costa Rica, I'd become well-known from the Atlantic coast to the Pacific. If anyone outside of Mike's restaurant mentioned that the *dueño de Onyx se va a escapar de* Costa Rica (the owner of Onyx is going to escape Costa Rica), there would have been a Tico police marching band waiting for me along the entire border. The Ticos would have spread the word so that they and their *primos* (cousins) could watch the competition between me and the police as I tried to escape—and they tried to save face by capturing me.

I finished the covert goodbye party drunk enough to not give a shit about the mosquitos.

Chapter 69

I WOKE EARLY ENOUGH TO SILENTLY SAY HELLO TO MY MACAW AND parakeet neighbors before they awoke, remembering how much I admired their freedom as they called out to the local people of Jaco, before they painted the morning sky with their multicolor rainbow. I sat in my usual position on the patio and watched the people who struggled to survive but somehow ate every day. I used to feel sorry for them, having to live in their Central American poverty, while I only had to order whatever I wanted from my restaurant's kitchen. Sometimes, when we'd needed a change of pace, we would choose from any of the restaurants in town and eat and drink whatever we wanted from the menu.

I had lost absolutely everything except my extremely damaged spirit. Fusion was the last solution I'd had left to give me the minimum to restart and rebuild my life. I had to walk away from it. No one, including Mike and his restaurant family, knew the plan, day, or time. I was mentally and physically a broken man who was trying to save his life to reunite with his family.

Mommy está pasando. My daughter's innocent words about my wife "pasando" danced in my head. Six months is a very long time to leave a beautiful young woman alone, and I just prayed to my guardians that I wasn't sitting on the final barn fire of destruction I'd successfully created in Central America. I made it a point to keep my plan completely hidden from my family. In case I didn't make it, I didn't want Cecy to worry or get involved with my backdoor exit out of Costa Rica. I knew the Costa Rican authorities would double or triple my time in jail if they caught me trying to leave the country without their permission.

I watched as the rainbow of macaws and parakeets returned to their perches; I wanted to say goodbye to them and my iguanas who'd been so generous in sharing their tainted rainwater with me from their homes on the restaurant roof. The rainbow was also my signal to grab the last possessions I could fit inside one suitcase, take the $2,500 from my secret hiding place, and walk briskly to catch the last bus out of Jaco to San José.

There was a little daylight left; it stayed long enough for me to see what would never be my life again. My heart pounded in pain as the bus passed by my ten-year-old son's home, knowing he would wake up tomorrow to find out his father was dead, in jail waiting for his death, or restricted from ever entering his country again.

The darkness was comforting. I didn't need to look out the windows; Costa Rica had been my home for fifteen years, and I knew exactly where I was just by passing a building under a streetlight or passing through a specific mountain range. I thought, *I truly love this incredibly beautiful country. Why doesn't it love me?*

The bus pulled into the depot at eight thirty. I rushed to get off the bus, grabbed my suitcase, and ran for the last bus to Limón, a city on the Atlantic coast. When I got to the gate, the bus was already pulling out. No matter what I did, it wouldn't stop. There I was, in the middle of San José with one suitcase, five months' worth of Tico blue-collar salary in my pocket, and no plan B. Joanna's wasn't an option; she would definitely have a happy hour buzz by this time of night and would probably not remember to keep my escape a secret. Her mixed gringo and Tico network would have spread the word throughout Costa Rica within twenty-four hours. The other option was losing a day and some gringo-escapee discretion by spending extremely valuable money on a hotel. I was well on my way to becoming stress's best friend.

"Taxi?" I heard someone speak behind me with a heavy Tico accent. I turned and saw a taxi with a driver who was very happy to double-charge this obviously frustrated gringo who was protecting his one suitcase with his life and get him to his destination.

I turned, and to his surprise, I said, "*Yo perdí el último autobus para Limón. Necesito estar allí esta noche*" (I missed the last bus for Limón. I need to be there tonight).

The taxi driver had not expected me to speak Spanish; he rebalanced his attitude and quickly said, "*Hay otra estación que tiene un bus para Limón que va a salir a las nueve. Vamos rápido; quizás logremos agarrar el autobús*" (There is another station with a bus for Limón that leaves at nine. Let's go quickly; maybe we'll arrive on time.)

I didn't hesitate getting into his taxi. In my position, I couldn't care less if he charged me three times the fare, as long as I was on that 9:00 p.m. bus to Limón. I had learned many things about Costa Rica and its culture, and I knew the situation I'd gotten myself into. Taking the last bus to the most dangerous city in Costa Rica was like skimming the Monarch Notes an hour before a class presentation.

Chapter 70

I JUST MADE THE NINE O'CLOCK BUS. I COULD HAVE KISSED THE TICO TAXI driver. I began the second leg of my escape journey.

I was sure the obviously hardworking young Nica sitting next to me on the bus was relieved to have a secretive gringo instead of an irritated Tico sitting next to her for the three-hour trip to the Atlantic coast. After the Contra and Sandinista war of the eighties in Nicaragua, Nicas migrated to Costa Rica in droves; many came from partial homes with dirt floors to find any job they could in Costa Rica, not just to have a better life for themselves, but also to help the families they left behind in Nicaragua. The Ticos were very frustrated with their Nica neighbors taking jobs from them. The gringos became educated on how the hungry, hardworking, and powerless Nicas were more focused than the Ticos. The Ticos effectively used their connections and laws to win most employer court cases against gringos. Cultural prejudice between the Ticos and Nicas was in full bloom.

The bus pulled into the Limón station at midnight. By the time I took my suitcase out of the luggage compartment, all the other passengers were gone. I had seen cockroaches disappear fast; the people on the last bus to Limón came in at a strong second. A light went off in my head as my ghetto instincts kicked in to tell me that I was a gringo who was alone in the most dangerous city in Costa Rica at midnight. *Wake the fuck up!* I thought. I had to figure out how to get to the hotel I had booked.

The bus station left one light on that shined on the spot I was standing with my one suitcase. I watched as two young men calmly approached me from the side with half smiles on their faces. I turned when I heard footsteps approaching me from the other side. It was a well-dressed black man walking directly to me from the other dark side of the station. I didn't have enough red flags to indicate that I was in a position that most people did not want to experience, especially in a third world country's most dangerous city.

"Where are you going?" the well-dressed black Tico man asked, knowing that there was a very tense situation at hand in the completely empty bus station. How would I have responded, being lost in an empty bus station, flanked by strangers, with five months' salary in cash in my pocket? I had no were to run; Limón was a labyrinth I was not able to navigate. A plethora of potential violent scenes danced around in my mind.

"I booked a hotel that is two blocks from this station. I will go to Puerto Viejo tomorrow," I replied. Once again, I'd given way too much information; gringos with money went to Puerto Viejo!

"We know where the hotel is," the young men said. They pointed at a street. "It's very close, a couple of blocks down there."

I took a quick look down the completely dark alley they directed my attention to. I unsuccessfully tried to paint a smile of confidence on my face while I turned to look directly into four eyes and answered, "¿Verdad?" (Really?).

The slick older man started to realize I was a man with enough Tico experience to know I was cautiously weighing my very uncomfortable options. "Amigo, I'm a taxi driver. Why spend your money on a hotel when I can take you tonight to Puerto Viejo?" he said. Financially that made sense, but I did not know him or observe one single taxi in the area. Costa Rica used to have more illegal "pirates" (regular Ticos with cars who claimed they were taxis) than legal taxis. By the time I had to graciously depart through the back door, the legal taxis had proven enough negative "pirate" cases to the courts to mostly eliminate their competition and monopolize their transportation charges, yet there were still a few "pirates" floating around. If New York taxi drivers had known how much the Tico drivers were charging, they would have started migrating south.

The competition heated up between the opportunist on my right and the ones on the left. The two young brothers decided to take it to the next level. They snatched my suitcase from my hands and said, "Follow us." They started walking down the dark alleys.

I don't remember how I got to them so fast; "ghetto" jumped into my heart, and my chest stuck out as I snatched my livelihood back from them. I looked them in the eyes and said, "I can handle this." In the ghetto, one always stuck their chest out to show pride—even if they were about to die. The two young men followed me back to the only light of the bus depot.

The taxi driver without a taxi repeated his offer of a one-hour drive to Puerto Viejo. After what had happened with the young brothers, my trust was definitely shifting in the other direction. Even though I didn't see a taxi, I decided to take the taxi driver's offer; I thought if worse came to worst, I had a better chance of surviving against the older taxi driver than the two young brothers.

Chapter 71

RAUL LED ME TO HIS TAXI. HE WAS ONE OF THE BEST-DRESSED TAXI drivers I had ever seen; his taxi was almost sterile inside and out. I put my suitcase in the trunk and jumped into the front seat. Ticos pride themselves on being one of the friendliest societies on this planet. It was now about one o'clock; the taxis usually added people on rides to increase their income, but we both knew he wasn't going to stop. If I had placed myself in the back seat of the taxi, it would have been a complete insult to a Tico, and in my precarious position, insulting people was not an option.

I was one of the most extroverted one-on-one persons I knew, and yet when I first got into Raul's taxi, I was the perfect emulation of a mute from the Dark Ages: nervous, scared, and paranoid. I was sure it wasn't difficult for Raul to notice my eyes dotting around and head tilting in order to view any and every mirror I had access to. I created my own visual perimeter of safety. I was on the cutting edge of schizophrenia as I kept a silent vigilance of every single vehicle that was in front of us, beside us, and especially behind us. I was well aware of the entrapment techniques that many thieves used to set up their victims.

When I look back, I smile at the thought of how Raul must have been quite amused observing my act in his car; he was a taxi driver at the border of Costa Rica and Panama and must have seen hundreds of nervous gringos with one suitcase and bribery money hidden somewhere on their bodies as they tried to escape the country.

After we drove for 20 minutes, Raul decided to devolve my nightmare into a bad dream. "Man," he said, "you know I don't just drive a cab; I have a specialty import and export business."

I continued to check my mirrors. I thought I knew exactly what he meant, and I thought, *He's a fucking drug dealer; if anyone can make me disappear, it's him.* I had learned one very important strategy after traveling to forty-five states and thirty-five countries: if you are in an uncomfortable situation with someone, be very respectful and make the person feel like a friend.

"I have a small problem with my son's mother," I said. "She's Argentinian, but she lives and has a business here." I stopped talking; giving a stranger a lot of information wasn't my plan.

Raul smiled at his success of relaxing my vocal cords. "Oh! I understand; I was in the same situation with my son's mother. She put me in jail too." Raul knew the exact position I was in at that special moment in my life—from the only sentence I had planned to give him.

I needed to trust someone. Raul was Afro-Caribbean and seemed to want to make friends with a brother from North America. If I was to take an educated guess, I think I may have been the first black gringo Raul had met who'd been desperate enough to risk his life to escape Costa Rica or any third world country.

I felt that the coast was clear when we passed the halfway mark to Puerto Viejo. I relaxed a little bit, and by the time I took a breath, Raul started to regret getting curious enough to open up a conversation with me. When I mentioned who the contact in my escape was, he got very serious. "Oh no!" he exclaimed. "You don't want to trust that man; you will end up back in jail. He's an ex-politician who is not to be trusted."

I was a little confused about why an exporter whom I'd just met knew about the person Mike and his family said I could trust. I was very confident Mike and his family would not set me up, but I had lived and been burned in Costa Rica for fifteen years. I had watched friends turn against friends and family for money, and I was acutely aware of the money I had in my pocket.

My very battered instincts told me to try to trust Raul. I was very disappointed, but Raul's attitude in his words showed that he genuinely believed an unscrupulous person had given me the contact. He convinced me to let go of this only contact I had to cross the Costa Rica border into Panama. My mind was getting so damn tired of fear and depression that it was almost completely numb. In my experience, life's sine wave's ups and downs were usually spaced out in three-to-six-month intervals; my sine wave at this point was a microwave.

"Tony, I know someone who works at customs. He can get you across and stamp your passport for $1,500," Raul said.

I waited to answer. I thought, *Of course my new import-export friend had a connection at customs.* I was not surprised that he was aware of the standard gringo illegal crossing price. There was nothing more valuable than my fifteen-year experience with the Tico culture and way of thinking to support my life-or-death decisions in my new escapee career.

"Raul, that sounds great," I replied. "I was very worried about being in Panama with an illegal passport. If they found out, they would send me back to Costa Rica—and who knows how long they would put me in jail for trying to escape. Let's do it."

Raul was pleased. I was trusting him with the $1,500 fee that would pay off every customs doorkeeper while leaving a very nice percentage for him since he would manage the project of getting me out of his country. "OK!" he declared. "I will set it up for tomorrow."

Raul and I drove for a while, sharing with each other our life's adventures in Costa Rica. It turned out he had lived a few years in New York, which gave third world people extra "life credits" in their native countries. I shared with him a few stories of my riches-to-rags adventures, to his complete amusement. I actually found myself laughing at the stories of how I had expertly fucked up my life. I told him about my beautiful wife and daughter who were waiting for me in Panama; he agreed that it would have been a bad idea to get their hopes up when there was a very big chance I would be seized on one of the sides of the border.

Mike suggested that I find a hotel close to where the contact who would help me cross the border was. It was dark and late, and I was tired. I just wanted a safe place to sleep.

Raul slowly but surely took me under his umbrella of protection. I wouldn't have trusted a butterfly at that point in my life. He turned to me, knowing my hotel was in Limón, and asked, "What hotel are you staying at?"

"I don't have one," I said. "I was going to stay in Limón one night and then stay at a hotel close to my contact in Puerto Viejo." I brought out the little paper. "My friends told me to find a hotel in this area until I made my contact with that person."

Raul hesitated for a moment; he knew that I was warming up to him but still was mentally unstable. "My friend has a hotel in Puerto Viejo. It's comfortable, and he will give you a good price, maybe around thirty or forty dollars. Are you interested?"

I automatically became uncomfortable; it was now my forte. It didn't take long to do the math. It was almost three in the morning, I was escaping, I didn't know a soul in Puerto Viejo, I had $2,500 in my socks, and I didn't have a hotel or room. "Sounds perfect!" I blurted out confidently.

By the time we entered Puerto Viejo, I had exceeded my amount of tolerable travel. I could not wait to get out of the taxi. All my stress wanted was alcohol. My paranoia had decreased to a normal heart attack level until Raul took a left turn onto a dirt road. It wasn't unusual for there to be dirt roads in Costa Rica, but I wasn't feeling very adventurous. I had expected to go to a hotel on or around the main strips in Puerto Viejo.

Raul continued to speak. The road was completely dark except for whatever flora and fauna the headlights revealed on the snake-formed jungle path. The journey to the hotel seemed to last forever—at least long enough for my paranoia to continue to rise. I felt I could trust Raul with my plight, but I never diverted for one second from the instinct of never trusting anyone with my life.

The ride finally ended when we took a quick right to face a twenty-by-ten-foot gate. A middle-aged black man was waiting to pull the gate open for us to enter. My trust level was still pretty low, but I was happy as hell to see a line of small hotel rooms directly one hundred meters from the gate.

I should have never watched those escape shows on TV; just like the 24/7 news channels, having watched them made all the shit I was going through smell twice as bad. I reminded myself that I'd walked seven miles through the Serengeti, scuba dived with sharks in Belize, and stood still during a blizzard after a Harvard University campus party while a drunk young man waved a Bowie knife at my stomach and threatened to stab me. These memories of bravery were not helping me with this particular situation; I felt like my emotions were being consistently and intensely squeezed by an iron corset.

Raul said, "George, this is Tony. Tony, this is my good friend, George, the owner of this hotel."

George and I greeted each other, and he led me directly to my room. I put my suitcase down before heading to the sitting area to rejoin George and Raul. As I passed the room next to mine, my seventeen years of Central American experience could easily surmise that the voices I heard were a mature gringo man and young Tica woman enjoying their time together. I was a little bit jealous.

The assortment of beers George had in the cabaña fridge was a very welcomed site. The Caribbean people on the Atlantic side were very warm and friendly to me. I didn't know, but I didn't think it was because I mixed into their base color scheme; I got the impression it was the way they handled many aspects of life in general with everyone.

Raul took over in the presentation of my situation and escape plan to George. Complimenting me as a good man, he told George about my businesses in Costa Rica, the corruption that had taken me down, and how a woman had sent me to jail for child support when I had nothing. I knew that any sensible native of Costa Rica would know I had no choice; to go to the main jail without any resources would more than guarantee my demise within the first thirty days.

The gringo guest eventually drove his friend home and returned to sit and have a beer with us under the cabaña. Mike, the gringo guest, didn't take long to catch up to my situation; he had been in Costa Rica for more than twenty years and was well-educated on the dictionary of gringo downfalls, of which I was the new shining-star poster boy. He knew that he needed to keep quiet because of how word spread in Costa Rica.

"Be ready to leave tomorrow morning at ten," Raul said as he stood up to leave.

I smiled and shook Raul's hand to firm up our agreement. The same thought continued to repeat itself in my mind: *If anyone can get me over that border, it would be my new import-export friend.*

After Raul left, George, Mike and I decided to go to a late-night club to listen to reggae music and watch beautiful women seduce the universe, moving their bodies in perfect time with the rhythm. It was a great way to celebrate my last night in the country I loved.

I was ready the next morning before the sun came up. I waited until George woke. He immediately made coffee before cooking a simple but deeply appreciated breakfast. It was low season; George's hotel was off the beaten path and had an extremely low occupancy rate, but he treated me as if I was in a five-star hotel. I was actually starting to trust my new friends. It was the first time since I had first left for Central America that I'd met people to whom I felt I could open up the Monarch Notes of my story.

By noon, Puerto Viejo's heat was making the cold beer in the cabaña's refrigerator too tempting. Raul was running a little late, but it didn't bother me. After seventeen years of living in Central America, I had no choice but to be patient with absolutely every aspect of Central American life, including the lateness. George, Mike, and I thoroughly enjoyed sharing stories of the funny adventures we had endured in Costa Rica. With each second that passed, my freedom pounded deeper inside my mind.

Raul returned through the big gate around one o'clock. I was not too pleased to see the frown on his face. George handed Raul some food, which he devoured in a short period of time, preparing to stomach what he had to say to me. It seemed as if George already knew the upcoming outcome of our feat.

Raul could hardly look at me as he began to talk. He slowly lowered head, shaking it from left to right, and said, "Tony, I'm so sorry, man. They changed the rules at the border. My friend is refusing to take a chance; he could lose his job and go to jail. I'm so sorry, man."

I couldn't reply in Spanish or English; it felt as if every word in my vocabulary went up in a puff of smoke along with my hope. I had made it to the edge of freedom, ready to feel the joy, hugs, and love of my family. I didn't know if it was my blood or my soul, but something inside me started melting from my head to my toes. I felt that every option I had to survive became null and void.

Raul watched as the dark spirits surrounded my aura. I had no tears left to cry. All I could do was look for a pen, pad, and candle so I could write the words in my mind; writing under candlelight in my dilapidated restaurant helped me build the protective mental wall I had become accustomed to, keeping myself from giving up what I had left.

Raul did everything he could to isolate the details of his import-export business from his new friend, yet I was sure he was making every effort to free me from Costa Rica's bondage. I was sure Raul remembered that he'd advised me to not use my initial contact, which added to his self-made obligation to get me across the border. I applauded his effort, even as the diversion of my trust from Mike's family to Raul started to linger in the part of my mind that pondered my survival decisions.

"I have an idea. I'll be back soon." Raul left without saying another word.

George, Mike, and I continued drinking beers with a lot less joy than we'd had before.

Chapter 72

RAUL RETURNED AT AROUND FOUR O'CLOCK IN THE AFTERNOON. I FELT like I'd been waiting for the results of a biopsy as I watched Raul's car pull up to the cabaña. Raul opened the car door, put one foot out, and shouted what now seemed like my middle name: "Let's go!"

Without a thought, I threw my suitcase in the backseat and sat down in the passenger seat. I could tell from Raul's expressions that he was a man on a serious mission; he had dedicated himself to getting me across the border by any means possible, and I wasn't going to say or do anything to stand in his way.

The car stopped at a little restaurant on the edge of the river that separated Costa Rica from Panama. Raul joined the other Ticos watching Saprissa play La Liga. I knew and was very happy that I would get zero attention, thanks to the Tico's religious devotion to the game. I observed the aggressive current of the river that separated me from my freedom, remembering Raul's stories of the many people who'd been swept away as they tried to swim to the other side. I thought of the times in my life when I'd come extremely close to death: my macho swim in New Hampshire, scuba diving in Aruba, and the riptide at the beach in Costa Rica. It was enough to keep the thought of swimming across the raging river that drained into the Atlantic Ocean completely off my list of escape options.

I watched Raul sit at the bar and simply fuse with the other Ticos, watching the soccer match and joining them in the hypnotic state that enveloped Costa Rica whenever La Liga played Saprissa. I had sometimes wanted to bring a whip to work when I had been running my restaurants during certain soccer events to keep my staff moving more toward the customers than the televisions. I had gradually started to join in on the energy of the soccer matches, especially when the little country of Costa Rica had their team become the giant killer at the 2004 World Cup. At this point, however, as the hours went by in the restaurant, I couldn't have been any less interested. I knew my life was in the hands of the people who were watching the soccer match. Like a rejected puppy, I sat on a lower bench at the other side of the restaurant, away from Raul and his friends, and stayed silent.

Hours passed. La Liga won the match, and I watched with frustration all the Ticos discussing the results. I was expecting Raul to come over to speak to me about the plan, but he was acting as if I wasn't there. I was trying to suppress how annoyed I was getting when, as if a silent bell had rung, everyone sprang into action.

The day had just turned into dusk when Raul turned to me and said, "Ready?"

Before I could complete a yes, a young Tico picked up my suitcase. "*Sígueme*," (follow me) he said as he hastily left the bar. I followed him outside to the steep hill that led to the river. The young Tico walked down the hill like he was a professional skier. I was slightly malnourished with a 25 percent muscle loss, and I must have looked like I was walking on hot coals.

The Tico uncovered a small outboard motorboat hidden in the bushes at the edge of the river, put my suitcase inside the boat, and pushed it out to the river in a matter of seconds. Being in my situation was proof enough that I hadn't been at the top of my graduating class, but I was intelligent enough to follow this young Tico's lead as quickly as I could.

Once again, those documentaries on television of gringos trying to escape third world countries haunted my mind as I watched the border guards' pace up and down the bridge, which was about two football fields away from our crossing point. I just wanted a magic potion to make myself invisible for thirty minutes, yet I didn't want to push it by asking for too many potions until I was sitting on one of the economy seats on a plane back to the US.

As the young Tico and I reached the Panama coast, a short and stocky indigenous man jumped into the water and grabbed the rope the young Tico had thrown. I felt as if our small boat had turned into a time machine during the course of our journey across the river. There had been a moment in the trip during which I had forgotten my plight as I watched a plethora of indigenous children swimming with overwhelming joy in minimal to no clothing. I knew that I was witnessing a culture that had endured thousands of years, and that knowledge made me feel true happiness for the first time in more than a year. The man who pulled our boat in seemed to be the father and the patriarch of the tribe. He brought the boat to a shallow enough point for me to reach the dry land with a small step. Before I could grab my very heavy suitcase, the patriarch lifted it like a feather and said, "*Siga.*" I was starting to understand that Raul was a real professional import-export businessman; everybody at each point along the trek had been well-informed of their responsibilities.

I knew my question-and-answer period had passed. I followed the indigenous patriarch up the riverbank, passing the huts of his village. The tribe was waiting patiently for the scheduled parade of the unnerved gringo escapee. I must have looked like a black deer in headlights as my six-foot body most humbly walked at the same height as my five-foot guide. I timidly waved and said, "Hola."

At the end of the village, a small path led to a thick jungle forest; inside, it was difficult to see more than three feet left or right. The sounds of the jungle inhabitants surrounded us as we showed total respect in every step we made in their precious home. I wanted to stop and observe the special reserve, but I could clearly sense that the patriarch had a schedule to keep. I pushed my fragile body to keep in step with his well-oiled human machine.

The hike through the beautiful jungle became long enough to make it annoying. Panama's dusk mosquitoes effectively formed battalions as they smelled the new blood; mine wasn't really new, but they seemed to like the fact that it was different. The mosquitoes completely turned off my nature-loving side as they threw a six-foot, two-hundred-pound dark-meat rave party on my body.

The small dirt jungle path instantly opened at the side of a two-lane highway. "Where's the taxi? There is supposed to be a taxi here!" Realizing the patriarch didn't understand one word of English, I quickly changed to Spanish. "*¿Dónde está el taxi?*" (Where's the taxi?). I tried to remain calm.

"No sé," (I don't know) the patriarch calmly responded. It was getting dark. I was sitting at the edge of the jungle with a three-quarters-naked man, and the promised taxi to my freedom was not there. My negative train of thought brought me to wonder exactly how many more minor heart attacks I would be able to endure before my body, mind, and soul decided it was best just to cash me in.

The taxi arrived fifteen minutes late. I realized then that having been married to a Panamanian for seven years, I should have known the taxi was going to be late.

A tall, skinny black man jumped out of the driver's seat like it was on fire. "Let's go," he said in solid English with a slight accent.

I walked across the street to the taxi to once again have my suitcase snatched from my hands. The man put it into the trunk of the taxi. "Sit up front," the driver commanded with pure immediatism in his words and mannerisms. My hands were tied, and my fate was out of them. I was at the least illegal in Panama, and I would do what I was told to do.

The taxi driver's mission was to take me to Changuinola so I could catch a bus to Panama City. I knew the bus made stops at Agua Dulce and La Divisa, where I would be able to make my way to Robles where my wife's family resided. Divisa was at least ten miles from Robles, and it would be almost impossible to hail a cab there. I would have to put my thumb out to complete my trip. Hitchhiking at four o'clock in the morning as a gringo in Panama would not be the greatest decision I had ever made; I would just add it to the pile of shit my life had become.

After only ten minutes into the taxi ride, I watched in horror as Panamanian border guards on the horizon grew into life-sized persons in the taxi's headlights as we approached. *What the hell is this?* I thought. *Raul told me that when we crossed the river, we would be past the guard station.* The crossing gates were down, blocking vehicles from passing through. The guards gave the hand signals that told the driver to slow down and my heart to speed up its beating.

I had no choice but to stay in my seat as my next heart attack played out. I went over my credentials: prisoner, escapee, illegal emigrant of Costa Rica, and illegal immigrant of Panama. I wondered if I had any more tricks up my sleeve, which I was sure had emptied at least a year ago. I could not stop paranoia from enjoying another opportunity to take me over again.

Were the border guards the last piece of the fifteen-hundred-dollar bribery puzzle? Would the players in my final Central American adventure send me back to a very long prison term in Costa Rica and take their share of the prize? Raul had seemed sincere; I hated doubting him, but I'd recently lost hundreds of thousands of dollars to a corrupt corporation, albeit a gringo corporation.

The taxi came to a stop at the checkpoint. If I had learned one thing in my seventeen years of life in Central America, it is that when you are in doubt, keep your mouth shut. I tried to act like I was an ignorant farmer going on a trip, even as I was acutely aware of my status as a gringo thinking his luck had just run out.

The taxi driver slowly opened the door. One guard with a serious face approached the taxi; another guard positioned himself at a distance behind the taxi close enough to get a clear look at my head.

As soon as the taxi driver had his door opened wide enough to get out, the serious officer threw what seemed to be a crunched chewing gum wrapper at the driver and said in English the words that set me free: "Get out of here."

I was ecstatic. I was not only free; the guards were either trained or updated enough to deal with various gringo situations, and as it seemed, they were trying indirectly to impress me with their English skills.

The taxi sped ahead to catch my bus at Changuinola. Panama didn't practice daylight savings time; it was religiously dark by six o'clock every night. I was exhausted with the fear emotion that dominated my new life. Many times, when I got small views of the thick layers of fauna that protected the jungle from too many outsiders, I would envision myself walking into the woods and laying down to let the animals eat me and relieve me of my emotional turmoil.

I was no longer in Costa Rica; I had illegally crossed the border into Panama. I didn't know how Panama would act if they found out a person who had been on his way to being arrested had crossed over their border illegally. I knew if Panama turned me back to Costa Rica, I would have been locked up in the big jail "until death did us part."

I sat quietly in the taxi, a little bit impressed with Raul's underground railroad. Except for the fifteen-minute lag after the jungle hike, everything had been planned so well. The taxi driver seemed to know he had to make up for the fifteen-minute delay by adding a few miles per hour to his speedometer.

We were both relieved when we saw the bus with a neon sign lit up with "Panama City" as its destination. The taxi driver parked right in front of the bus's path just in case the bus tried to move.

I flung open my door open to rush to buy a ticket when the driver stopped me and put his hand on my shoulder. "Give me forty dollars and wait here," he said firmly.

I was a little annoyed at what I thought would be a surcharge on the fifteen hundred dollars I had already paid to Raul to give me the best opportunity to live until I arrived at my Panamanian in-laws' house. I'd been told that the ticket to Panama would only be twenty dollars, but my spirit had evolved into putty, so I accepted my subservient position. I just wanted to survive my personal nightmare.

The bus was fifty feet from where I found an empty bench to act incognito. There were way too many people and officers running around the station for comfort. I was becoming more stressed and paranoid as each minute passed. I don't remember if it was fifteen, thirty, or forty minutes that the taxi driver was at the ticket office, but it was way too long.

The driver finally came out, handed me a ticket, pointed to the bus, and said, "There's your bus. Goodbye, my friend."

I jumped out of the car, grabbed my suitcase, which was now my best friend, and was, for the first time in my life, happy to sit in the back of the bus. Before the bus left, I looked at my ticket, curious to confirm whether or not I'd succumbed to a twenty-dollar surcharge. I opened my ticket, making sure I was sitting in the correct seat. The seat was confirmed for a "Mr. Anthony Chang." A much-needed smile of satisfaction engulfed my face.

Chapter 73

I WAS HAPPY TO NOT HAVE ANOTHER PASSENGER NEXT TO ME. I HAD room to spread out and pretend my skittish mind would let me sleep. It was pitch-black outside. I wanted to see the lush Caribbean forest that lined the highway to Panama City, but it wasn't in the cards. I decided to contemplate all the mental and physical conversions my family and I had endured in the past year. I was trying to offload some of the fear I had compiled over the previous thirty days of my life, and it was like putting a very thin pin needle into a high-quality air mattress. I felt like I will look like a deer in headlights to my wife; she was very confident in her independent survival skills. I wondered if I had stayed away from them too long, and I asked myself whether I'd given a beautiful woman who was now used to a good life too much time to reevaluate her options. Who did "Mommy pasó" with? I had gathered the extra strength I had needed to survive the past few months from my love of my family, the support of my friends, and the care of Mike. I had needed all three to gather the courage to risk my life crossing the border.

The bus slowed down and came to a stop after about three hours of the trip. I was confused. I looked out of the window and only saw the dark of the night speckled with very few streetlamps. During three of the eight-hour trips I'd taken to Panama, the bus had stopped at well-lit bus stations to pick up passengers, and also one very busy restaurant for a short break and meal. I was very frustrated at this extra stop in the middle of nowhere. I thought that, like all the taxi and public bus drivers seemed to do in Panama City, the bus driver was stopping at his or a relative's house for a snack or conversation. I thought, *I really don't need this shit at this point.*

The driver opened the door. To my surprise, he didn't move. The customs police did, though, as they slowly climbed the three steps to enter the bus, writing the beginning to my newest nightmare.

The police took a couple of steps forward and asked random people for their identification. I tried to be as subtle as possible as I watched the border guards make their way down the aisle of the bus toward my seat in the back. I tried to think of a plan, but I had nothing except that my name was Anthony Chang. The only Chinese person I knew was Bruce Lee, my real name was on what was now my illegal passport, and I had crossed the border without permission.

The closer the border guards came, the more ways I tried to make myself invisible. Thank God I was a black man in a country whose natives were the complete range of the color spectrum. I spoke great "I am a gringo" Spanish; I planned to keep my mouth shut at all costs.

One of the policemen walked up to my seat before turning away from my seat and heading down my row of chairs to the back. He turned his head and checked another row. I wondered if he could smell or feel the extreme fear from the man who was looking directly at the loaded gun on his hip. I began to sweat on the air-conditioned bus just before both policemen turned around and walked off the bus.

Chapter 74

ALTHOUGH DIVISA WAS LOCATED ABOUT TWENTY MILES FROM ROBLES, where my in-laws lived, it was the closest official bus stop for cross-country buses. However, I remembered observing some of the cross-country buses stopping in places in Robles. I had lived in Central America long enough to understand that the local families and their friends were given special privileges in many places. I really didn't want to wave down a four-in-the-morning taxi, much less hitchhike from Divisa to Robles, even though hitchhiking was still prevalent in Central America.

Divisa was a major checkpoint, and it was crawling with customs agents; if I disembarked the bus at Divisa at four in the morning and proceeded to walk down the road, I could possibly raise a lot of red flags in the very experienced minds of the customs officers. I realized after the three surprise custom officers' boarding that they were actually looking for a specific profile. One can almost sue for profiling in the first world—but not in the third. I decided to take a chance and stay on the bus through the Divisa customs check and work on my Spanish to ask the driver as politely as I could to let me off at Robles.

I knew that from Divisa to Robles was a thirty-minute drive during normal hours; there was no traffic, and this bus driver was driving like he was at the Indy 500. Ten minutes after we left Divisa, I walked the tightrope to the front of the bus, saluted the driver's helper, and looked at the driver with the utmost respect directly in his eyes. "*¿Por favor, puedes parar en Robles?*" (Please, can you stop in Robles?)

In the many third world countries I had visited, especially in Africa, they would ignore you at the sound of this type of question. At first, I was offended by the people staring at me and my family, but after my seventeen-year stint in Central America, I realized that this was directly related to communication and respect.

The bus driver, pleased that his black gringo surprise passenger could actually speak Spanish, did not hesitate to smile and say: "Si, mi amigo," (Yes! my friend) after he caught his breath.

The bus stopped under the crossover bridge in Robles one hundred yards from Cecy's family's home. I thanked the driver in my best Spanish and walked down the stairs, where the helper had already opened the luggage compartment door so I could pull out my suitcase. *"Hasta luego,"* (See you next time) the helper said to me.

"Hasta luego," I said as my spirit filled with a sense of happiness and accomplishment.

My walk to my in-laws' house was not like any walk I had ever taken. It was a march with my own band following me with all the brass, string, and percussion. This haggard middle-aged man was celebrating the freedom from his Costa Rican chains. I wasn't in the secure arms of my home country yet, but I was one large step away from eating the roach-filled jail food and the very high risk of being killed in one of the worst jails in Central America. The only bad note that entered the crescendo of the music, no matter how loud the band played, was my love for my beautiful son I was leaving behind.

Everyone at my in-laws' house was asleep with no idea I was lying in my favorite hammock in the backyard. Ernaldo, a close friend of Cecy's father who was actually more like family to him, eventually emerged from his very small *cabina,* which Cecy's father had built in the backyard. Ernaldo was happy when he realized that I wasn't a *ladron* (thief). He looked at me with a smirk and said, *"¿Por qué no llamaste?"* (Why didn't you call?).

I smiled and said, *"Yo no sé,"* (I don't know), knowing why.

Ernaldo turned around and returned to his cabina without saying another word.

Chapter 75

ONE BY ONE, THE FAMILY LOOKED OUT THE BACK DOOR TO VERIFY THAT the flesh of their lost gringo was real. One of the last ones to see my unhealthy body was my favorite sister-in-law, Jan-Sue. She was my *hermanita* (little sister), friend, and confidante. Every time I went to Robles, my eyes would scan each house and the town for her presence. Jan-Sue spent a split second greeting me and ran off to inform her big sister that I was actually at their home.

The family was in shock; they wanted to ask me a million questions, yet they restrained themselves because they knew I did not fully understand their "interior" Spanish (country Spanish). It was in their best interest to inform Cecy, who was on vacation with her aunt, and wait for her return in order to get a complete picture of her husband's sudden appearance back into their lives.

My last bite of my mother-in-law's very welcomed breakfast was absorbed just in time for Cecy, her aunt, and my Lucy to arrive from their Parasi vacation house. Cecy ran to me and jumped into my arms; joy filled my heart because I'd had no idea how the wife I adored was going to react to my sudden appearance. Many doubts had filled my mind between the time I'd heard the words "Mommy está pasando" and the time of my arrival.

Cecy's aunt stood in the background, posing like a boss who'd given her protected workers a special treat. Cecy moved to the side to make space for one of the most special people to me on this earth. My Lucy could not move; she looked at me with fascination as if I was a ghost, a spirit, or Mickey Mouse. My heart ignited with the pure love I had for my little angel as I patiently waited for her to realize I was not holographic. I noticed a bubbly rash on the side of her face before she leaped, crying, into my arms. I was immediately concerned about the rash, but I temporarily excused it in order to not spoil that special moment. Cecy joined into the family hug to complete the circle.

Chapter 76

I GRABBED MY ONE AND ONLY SUITCASE, SAID MY GOODBYES TO EVERYONE else at the house, and jumped into the rental car with my family.

Cecy sat in front with her aunt, and I rode in the back with Lucy, enjoying every minute of the family reunion.

Lucy, realizing her father wasn't a dream or a ghost, demanded 99 percent of my attention, which I was happy to give her.

My wife turned to smile at us every now and then, but she gave me minimal conversation.

"What is that rash on Lucy's face?" I asked.

"What rash are you talking about?" Cecy responded.

"When Lucy came out of the car to hug me in Robles, there was a bubbly rash spot on her face."

Cecy turned the lights on in the dark car and asked Lucy to turn to her. "There's no rash," she said after inspecting our daughter's face. Cecy looked confused at my assertion.

When I looked at Lucy in the light, I saw that the rash was gone. I pointed to the exact place I had seen the rash. "It was there. I saw it." Cecy turned back around to finish her conversation with her aunt.

We arrived at the vacation home on the beach late at night and instantly proceeded to set up our sleeping quarters for the night. Lucy had a bed in the living room on the first floor. We opened the sleeper couch and made it up for me to use. The sleeper couch seemed like a top-of-the-line beauty rest mattress to this malnourished man who had spent the past six months on thin mats strategically laid out on chairs and a broken, thirty-degree-tilted maid's bed.

I was tired but too excited to sleep. I could hear Cecy and her aunt having one of their marathon conversations. An hour passed. I checked on Lucy, who was asleep with the angels; the conversation on the second floor was not loud enough to reach the first floor where she was sleeping. I was tired and becoming a little irritated looking at the empty side of what I thought was our queen couch bed.

Two, then three, hours passed, and I arrived at the realization that my wife, whom I hadn't seen in six months, did not want to sleep beside her husband. "Mommy está pasando" were the words that ran through my mind before I finally slept with my demons.

Chapter 77

It was a long and puzzling ride back to Panama City. Lucy wanted so much more of my attention than her mother did. No matter what had happened with my wife in the past six months, my family was all I wanted and needed in order to move forward with my life.

Cecy would turn from the front seat every now and then to throw one of her beautiful smiles my way. I appreciated her efforts. The ride gave me flashbacks of my vacations with the Torreys. All the kids would sit in the back of the family's Volkswagen van, playing games, and the eldest daughter would sing a folk song. My godmother would join in on the songs and periodically look back at us with the same smile that Cecy was giving me.

After we arrived back at Cecy's grandmother's house, I could tell our relationship was gliding in neutral. Cecy continued to stay close to her aunt. Cecy did not sleep with me the night we returned to her grandmother's house in Panama. The next day, I confronted my wife. I wasn't surprised when she told me that she was uncomfortable with being intimate with me until I took a blood test. I understood her concern; I had been in Jaco, Costa Rica's "devil's playground." I went straight to the clinic to clear both of our heads, wondering why we didn't partner on this wonderful adventure.

All my tests came back negative, which relieved us both, but that did not clear Cecy's mind. Her energy of extremely focused love had changed directions. I tried to put a smile in front of my frustrations. Cecy basically treated me like a puppy on a leash every day I plotted to return to North America. She had secured a position as a writer in the media business with TVN News in Panama City and was now the breadwinner.

Cecy showed no sensitivity toward my illegal presence when she decided to bring me along with her to complain about crowd control to the police chief at Carnaval in Panama City. I would have been more comfortable at Carnaval if it hadn't consisted of a hundred thousand people and a thousand policemen.

I was a nervous and broken man who now had to depend on a wife who had been consistently blinking the hazard lights of our relationship ever since we had decided to return to Costa Rica. I contemplated the decision I had made to leave an income of one hundred thousand dollars per year, a thirty thousand-dollar expense account, and a company car to have my ass handed to me in Central America. I had to put all my haunting thoughts aside; I was now part of a family with a child who deserved the best. I had to accept the new realities of the relationship I had with my wife. I metamorphosed into her puppy and had to follow her, wagging my tail and acting like I was happy.

A car of young Panamanian men passed us one time when we were leaving her grandmother's house to once again try to enjoy ourselves, and one man screamed out the window and called Cecy his sister-in-law. I looked toward my wife, who used to be offended when men would not respect her wedding ring, and watched as she laughed at their advances, appreciating the flattery.

Chapter 78

"WE HAVE TO GO TO DIVISA TO FINISH SIGNING THE APPROVAL ON THE transfer for the car you gave to my uncle José," Cecy said. "You can say goodbye to the family then—just in case you get the money to leave." Her words were my confirmation of my now very low position on Cecy's totem pole.

It took me a second to answer my new wife. *Really! Really! And really!* Having to go with an illegal passport to customs police headquarters to sign off on a car was not exactly what I wanted to hear. I knew that Cecy's family knew my situation. I had no idea how I would make any more space in my collection of fearful events, but I knew I had to go to the office and place my freedom at the mercy of Cecy's family's instincts.

My basic blood test, the donated car mechanic fees for the car I had given to José, and the customs expenses of legalizing the Costa Rican car in Panama had depleted my plane ticket money. I had one very unstable wild card left in my phone number list.

Armando was a great person and the epitome of entrepreneurship; we had been neighbors during the good times when I had lived in the Panamanian high-rise. Armando was married to a wonderful woman with three children and spent every minute of his life trying to come up with a plan to make them extremely comfortable. Being an entrepreneur myself, I understood the extreme ups and downs a person endured while trying to achieve their dream. I had loaned Armando $1,500 during one of his "down" times; I was hoping deep in my soul that he was having an "up" time when I asked him to pay his debt back to me so I could return to the States to rebuild my life.

"No problem, Tony. I'll have it for you tomorrow," he replied. Armando knew the position I was in and could only think of returning the loan to his loyal friend. Up to this very day, I don't know what financial position Armando was in at that time, yet he gave me the $1,500 the next day. Even though Armando was settling a debt with me, he joined Mike on the pedestal of my lifelong friends and heroes.

Chapter 79

CECY'S PARENTS, UNCLE CHICO, UNCLE JOSÉ, AND AUNT CHEFE WERE my entourage and support system that caravanned with me to transfer my car to the family at the Divisa customs checkpoint. Cecy's family knew that if this regional-manager-turned-fugitive met with the twenty-plus border patrol officers alone, he would probably never return. Even though I was broke, I had some minimum but valuable use to the family left. Chefe and José wanted my Kia Sportage, and Cecy's mother wanted to save Lucy's family. Thus, Cecy's father and uncle Chico wanted to protect me from being arrested or deported back to Costa Rica.

My nightmare was far from over. During the drive, my mind streamed a large variety of possible scenes that could take place during this continuing horrible time in my life. The Divisa was border police heaven. My passport was illegal. The Kia meant nothing to me; the main reason I was willing to risk my freedom once again was because Cecy's family thought I could get my passport stamped from the sale of the car.

When we got there, the police were curious but not surprised that a gringo was giving a local family a car. They were curious because Cecy's family came in numbers, and usually it would be just the young girlfriend or wife who would accompany the gringo's supportive efforts to please her.

It took some time to sign all of the forms to transfer the Kia. When the police finally asked for my passport, depression poured over and covered me like a five-star hotel's shower. The way I handed the passport to the officer would have made any New York cop cuff me right away. This border officer had enough experience to give me a quick look over his shoulder as he walked away, expressing his interest in the manner in which I had given him the passport.

There were only ten people in the office, but my blurred psychotic vision saw at least twenty. One of the administrators made copies of my passport. When she was done, she handed my passport to the officer who was processing the paperwork, and I watched as she looked at me and said something to the officer. I just wanted to lay on the floor with my legs apart and my hands completely stretched to the sides and ask the Lord to just take me there and then.

The main officer called a conference with the entire office far enough away from the family's ears for us not to be able to hear anything. I think the conference lasted only five minutes to legal people; to me, it seemed more like five hours. Finally, the main officer walked to his desk, opened the drawer, pulled out his ink set, and stamped my passport.

Cecy's family, the officer, and I all knew what had just happened, but we did not say a word. Everyone smiled at each other.

Chapter 80

"ELLA NO VA." (SHE'S NOT GOING).

It was the night before I would return to Panama City to arrange my trip back to the States. It was one of those rare times when I was alone with Abuela (Grandma). Cecy and the other ladies of the family were having their own private conference inside the house. Abuela was the true matriarch of the family; everything centered around her, even when Abuelo (Grandfather) had been alive.

"¿Quien no va?" (Who's not going?)

Abuela looked up at me with a very serious look and said, "Cecy *no va a Estados Unidos.*" (Cecy is not going to the United States). I was in shock; I had presumed that going to the United States was my family's objective. I had planned on going first, to make enough money to bring my wife and baby to the States, and now I was hearing from the most important person in Cecy's life and someone who I had grown to love and respect that Cecy did not want to be with me in the United States.

Abuela's Spanish was mixed with Robles slang; most of the time, Cecy had to translate her words in order for me to understand her complete sentences. I focused everything I had learned about the Spanish language to make sure I was hearing Abuela's warning correctly. *"¿Por qué no?"* (Why not?)

Abuela gave me the international motion everyone understands, her head tilted toward her shoulder, the arms bent up, turning her hands upside down. I knew it was my problem.

Chapter 81

CECY, LUCY, AND I TRAVELED BACK TO PANAMA CITY AFTER THAT extremely interesting Robles vacation. Armando met us at the bus stop and returned the $1,500 I had lent him in the past. I was worried about his situation, but I had to selfishly accept the money of freedom.

We met with Cecy's closest friend, Yannisse, and her daughter at the Albrook mall. I had first met Yannisse when my buddy Alberto had invited Cecy and her to join me and my beautiful Ukrainian exotic dancer girlfriend at Carnaval, putting the actual woman I was in love with in a first-class observation seat for my newest romance.

Yannisse was a solid person and contained one of the warmest and realest hearts a person could possess. When she had joined Cecy and me at the beach ten years ago, walked the two of us into the shallow water, and prayed for our union, I had given her my love and respect as a true friend for life. The part of Cecy and Yannisse's relationship that would have gotten my vote for the Guinness Book of World Records was the length of their conversations; as soon as they lit their conversational fire, I would leave to find something of interest that would occupy me for a few hours.

There was a casino at Albrook mall, and while Cecy and Yannisse chatted away in super-fast Panamanian Spanish, I decided to entertain myself inside the casino. I entered the casino and scanned the small smoke-filled room; to my disappointment, there were no game tables. I knew how to always break even or win in blackjack as long as I didn't have a fifth drink. There was a time I had been complaining in an empty New Orleans bus about consistently losing, and the bus driver, having heard enough, looked over his shoulder, and said, "You need to know the rules." He then began educating me thoroughly.

I decided to play the auto-rob-you roulette wheel. As I played a few games, I became increasingly impressed with the old constantly smoking gringo at one end of the tables; he captured my fascination because he was the poster boy representing many failed expatriates, especially me in my present situation. As I watched the old gringo, I contemplated my life and how all of my actions for the past seventeen years had made a path to my personal hell. I use to arrogantly preach that hell wasn't below; people made their own hell. I was right! The old gringo was positioned to be one of my Ebenezer Scrooge spirits, the ghost of my future. I watched the old gringo, who could have easily been the father of the now missing drug-addicted Gringo Ghost whose needle turned him into Carry Grant. Without a change of expression, he put his losing bet on the electronic roulette table. I knew deep down inside that I was well along my journey to being him.

The next day, I would return to the United States of America, the home of the free, with a mission to rebuild my life and bring my family back together. My father's side of the family had contacted me. They knew all about my successes and failures. I accepted my cousins' support. It was a strong base on which to glue all my broken pieces back together, and it was absolutely necessary for me.

As we left the Armonk mall, I had tunnel vision all the way to the airport. The night before my flight had been a blur of wondering what else could go wrong.

Armando drove my family and me to the airport.

I hugged and kissed Cecy and Lucy after I exited the car outside the airport, determined to reunite with them ASAP. I loved them very much, but I wanted to get my ass home. I was ecstatic to have finally made it to the airport. I confidently walked to the ticket counter and handed the clerk my ticket and passport. I could have kissed my ticket and boarding pass when they were handed to me. I was more than happy to sit for five hours like a sardine in my economy seat. I walked to the security line to check my carry-on.

A customs agent standing in front of the scanner that checked the carry-ons was checking passports and tickets. I was starting to feel quite confident, especially since they had put my passport through the system at the ticket counter—and since it had an updated stamp from Panama's Divisa customs office.

I handed my passport and boarding pass to the customs agent before I went to the scanner, and he returned them to me after looking them over. I didn't see what happened behind my back as I passed through the body scanner, but the customs agent must have sent a special signal that I had missed. To my horror, another customs agent was waiting for me when I picked up my carry-on on the other side of the scanners.

"Mr. Florence?" she said.

"Yes," I replied while I once again felt depression melt around my mind and soul. I tried to not acknowledge or face it as my true reality, but I'd had to cover up and put makeup over my depression for the past two years. I'd had to continuously produce pictures of my children in my mind and write notes to keep myself from giving up and returning to dust.

"Follow me please."

I followed and sized up the female customs agent. She was short and stocky, and she had a gun.

I was led to an upstairs office that was empty. "What's the problem?" I asked, playing the stupid gringo. She flipped through my passport and showed me a different stamp than the updated one customs had given me at the Divisa office.

"Your stamp has been expired for a very long time," she said.

I maintained my stupid gringo role. "Yes, but my stamp was updated at Divisa," I pointed to it. "See? Right here." I tapped on the stamp defiantly, mostly because I was very nervous.

"Divisa has nothing to do with our department," she replied.

The little bit of spirit I had left sank into my Air Force sneakers. I was right back where I had started.

"Please wait here," the officer said as she left the room.

They would know that I had crossed the border illegally. They could either take me to a lethal Panamanian jail or send me back to Costa Rica. I had no more resources. Costa Rica would lock me up in their worst jail for a very long time. I was sure there would be additional time for escaping their country. I made the decision that all of the above was unacceptable.

I had dreamed about what my ultimate escape decisions would be for a while. These dreams were the answers to my life's what-if.

I created scenarios in my mind of what I would do to save or risk my life. I began to seriously think that I was out of options and had nothing to lose. I knew they would come in twos to deal with a big guy like me. I was out of shape, but I was still stronger than the average Joe. I imagined two officers entering the room, one standing immediately at my left and the other to my right. As soon as they got close enough, I grabbed both of their guns. I knew they would use their hands to wrestle their guns out of mine. This gave me an advantage because they were not able to reach for their sticks or another weapon. "Argh! Argh! Argh!" I screamed like a crazy man to keep them off-balance.

One of the officers finally lost his grip and backed off with his hands up, while the other officer continued to struggle with me to protect his gun. It was too late. I only needed one. I bet the officer who still had his gun felt helpless as the crazy gringo put the gun to his head.

I seriously contemplated the thin line between sanity and insanity as I waited in the office for the results that would set the trajectory of my next destiny.

The female customs officer returned alone. She gave me a serious look, hesitated long enough for my well-oiled paranoid mind to think more officers were about to follow her into the room, walked over to her desk, and pulled up the screen on her computer to support her claim that my visa tourist limit in Panama had expired six months ago. The two hundred-dollar fine to freedom was the rest of the money I had, but I was very happy to give the two hundred dollars and any change I had in my pocket to her.

Chapter 82

I APPRECIATED THAT MY SEAT WAS BY THE WINDOW. IF AN ANGEL LOOKED at my face through the window, it would have seen my face emulating the emoji with the wide-eyed surprised look on its face. I was very tired, but there was no way I could sleep. I was almost free. I didn't know when and where we crossed the various country borders; I just wanted to cross mine. Even at the point at which I started recognizing the USA border, I still felt I could be sent back. I was now at the mental place of trusting nothing and no one.

The plane landed in San Francisco, and I walked down the short dryer-exhaust-tube hallway, still not believing I might be free. Baggage claim was down a few escalators, and I carefully checked the LED signs for my flight number. My one suitcase came down the slide and seemed to move toward me with caution. I didn't move as I waited for everything I had left to trust me to do a better job of protecting it from the entities that had taken the rest of its family and friends.

My cousin Donny had instructed me to call him when I had my baggage, so I called him as I walked out of the airport. I had no idea what my future would bring as the warm San Francisco night breeze hugged me and tried to reassure me I was at the right place. I was a broken man; I no longer had the arrogance of the semi-successful preppy boy who'd won one of the most prestigious awards in the Boston public school system. I felt like my one suitcase and I were trying to avoid any spotlights that would expose my sadness and shame as I migrated to this promising country with many opportunities for the right person to build a new life.

9 781982 272128